Can We Do That?!

Outrageous
PR Stunts
that Work?!

Can We Do That?!

Peter Shankman

John Wiley & Sons, Inc.

Published by John Wiley & Sons, Inc., Hoboken, New Jersey.

Published simultaneously in Canada.

For general information on our other products and services or for technical support, please contact our Customer Care Department within the United States at (800) 762-2974, outside the United States at (317) 572-3993 or fax (317) 572-4002.

Wiley also publishes its books in a variety of electronic formats. Some content that appears in print may not be available in electronic books. For more information about Wiley products, visit our web site at www.wiley.com.

ISBN-13: 978-0-470-04392-9 (paper)

ISBN-10: 0-470-04392-X (paper)

Printed in the United States of America.

10 9 8 7 6 5 4 3 2 1

CONTENTS

?!

Thanks to all of my ghostly companions, ones who didn't kick me out but instead helped a curious girl learn her craft.

ACKNOWLEDGMENTS

?!

Thanks to all of my clients, especially those who didn't kick me out after I spewed forth some truly insane ideas.

BS and SWM, thanks for being my mentors. Everyone needs one; I got so incredibly lucky to have you both.

Thank you JH for believing in me from the start, and never ever stopping, even when I gave you reason to.

To my employees over the years, I hope I've kept it fun.

Thanks to my editor, Emily Conway, for emailing me one day out of the blue and saying, "So have you ever thought of writing a book?"

Finally, Mom and Dad, thanks for . . . wow, I don't even know remotely where to start. It would double the size of the book. So just . . . thanks. I love you both.

Can We Do That?!

?!

CHAPTER 1

Who Am I, and Why the Heck Should You Listen to Me?

You probably don't know me from Adam, but I am known. The media knows me, and more importantly, they know my clients. So I'm here to tell you why you should listen to me.

So you've bought this book. (Or you're sitting on the floor at a bookstore reading it while sipping a latte.) Either way, you're looking for a different way, a better way of marketing your company, your business, or yourself. You've listened to all the "PR Professionals," the "Publicists," and maybe even taken a course or two.

You've learned how to craft a press release and fill it with your latest company news or events. You've come up with a catchy boilerplate and made sure you listed the right contact information. You double-checked the date in the first paragraph, and confirmed all the numbers with your CFO.

You spent a week writing the release, got it cleared by your company lawyers, got a quote from your CEO, printed it on company letterhead, and sent it out to all the editors and reporters in your city.

Finally, it's the moment of truth. Your company has earth-shaking news, a major announcement. You're ready to tell the world.

And then you wait.

And the tumbleweeds blow by your desk, and the crickets chirp.

And there's not one story.

And you're left explaining why—to your bosses, to your shareholders, to your partners, to your clients.

This is not fun. In the PR world, the scientific term for what you're going through is, "This sucks."

We've all been there. The town of No Press. It's a lonely place, full of confused publicists who thought they could make it on a press release alone. It's like a retirement home for PR people who didn't have what it took. Meanwhile, journalists, savvy publicists, and the public are all watching, shaking their heads, saying, "He sent a press release addressed to 'Dear Editor.' He never had a chance."

Fortunately, there is a better way. Back in 1998, I started a small PR firm out of my apartment with one computer, one desk, and one cat. In eight years, the firm has handled PR, marketing, and events for some of the biggest companies out there—American Express, Disney, Juno Online Services, Richard Simmons, The Discovery Channel, as well as some of the smallest—Flying Fingers Yarn Shop, The Scott-e-Vest, the Bla-Bla.com ad network, and a ton of others. Big or small, household names or startups, they've all had one thing in common—they've had very successful public relations and marketing campaigns produced by my firm, The Geek Factory, Inc. These campaigns have generated revenue, exposure, and growth, sometimes beyond their (and our) wildest dreams. In this book, I show you what we did, how we did it, and how you can create those kind of results yourself.

There's only one rule I ask of you as you read and then apply what you've learned here:

Don't be afraid to be different.

Ask my parents. They'll both tell you that from the second I was born (way late and upside down) I always liked to do things differently. Sometimes I'd come home crying and tell my mom that the other kids didn't like me. She'd say that it wasn't that they didn't like me, they just didn't understand me, because I did things differently. I "marched to the beat of a different drummer," as she phrased it. She told me that one day my uniqueness would help me in the grown-up world. She promised one day I'd find out that not being like everyone else would come in handy.

Of course, like moms usually are, she was right; two successful companies, obscene amounts of media, and tons of satisfied clients later, I'm happy to have strayed from the pack.

At the time, though, I thought she was totally and completely out of her mind. I mean, come on—when you're 11 years old, not being like everyone else is a death sentence. Find me one kid who wants to be "different" at age 11. You can't. No one wants to be different when they're young. Hell, the majority of us don't want to be different now that we're older. But that's the true death sentence, in both business and life. You *need* to be different. Different gets you remembered, not simply recalled. Different gets the recognition and praise heaped on you, and not someone else.

Here's a secret: because the majority of people out there are afraid to be different, it allows people like us to own the ball game, the playing field—hell, the whole damn stadium—as long as we're just a little bit better, a little more distinctive. Be a little bit different, and you'll soar. People will notice. The media will write about you. The world will be your oyster, and all those other trite sayings. You'll be King of the World, or your little corner of it, anyway.

Quick quiz: Who will you remember more: the office mate who sends you a memo properly formatted; on white paper; with the correct subject, heading, and subhead, or the one who drops you an email that says, "Hey, wanna get with you on this project—can I buy you a burger later and talk?"

The answer is obvious. Burger Man will almost always win.

Be different. Be Burger Man.

It's being different that got me where I am, and gotten my clients the successful notoriety they've experienced. It's what put Bacardi on the top of the "Yahoo Most Emailed Photos" page, and what got Flying Fingers Yarn Shop a three-page spread in *The New Yorker*. It's what put RegisterFree.com on the front page of CNN.com, and New Frontier Media in the *Wall St. Journal*. It's what got me personally in *USA Today* and on CNN, more than once.

Being different has gotten me virtually all the PR, marketing, and for that matter, personal success I've had so far. It's also been the cause of some of my most spectacular disasters. But learning from them is half the fun.

OBJECT LESSON: WHO DO YOU REMEMBER?

You're on a crowded subway. It's packed full of people. You're standing, holding onto the handrail, drifting off into space, waiting for your stop. Virtually everyone looks the same, right? Try really looking at people tomorrow. It doesn't have to be on the subway—could be the freeway, the supermarket, the park, wherever you are where there are a ton of other people. They all sort of merge into one faceless, nameless person: "the crowd."

Well, there's a reason for that. Your brain simply can't process every single person you come in contact with on a daily basis. And why should it? We're all born with the spectacular instinct to *dismiss the banal*. If it bores us, serves no purpose, doesn't help us run our lives, do our jobs, or be happier, we tend to dismiss it. Every other car on the highway? Not important to us, other than the one in front of us we don't want to slam into. Other people on the subway? Who cares? They're not impacting our life in any way; we don't need to process them.

But, imagine. . . . You're on the freeway and out of the corner of your eye, you notice a fire-engine-red Lamborghini speeding up in your rearview mirror. You notice how low to the ground it is. You see the shiny, freshly waxed coating of paint. You admire the sleek, smooth lines on the car. It roars past you. You hear the purr of the engine as it gracefully hugs the road. You stare at it, you process it, you take it all in.

That car is a basic example of something out of the ordinary. You didn't expect to see a $175,000 car drive by you on your morning commute into the office, did you? Of course not. You expected to see Honda Civics, SUVs, and the like. So seeing something like a Lamborghini made you take notice. You remembered it. You're probably going to get into the office and tell your coworkers: "Guess what I saw this morning on the I-10!"

Hey, there's nothing wrong with a Honda Civic. It's a good quality car. But it's not a Lamborghini. You're not going to remember the 30 Honda Civics you saw this morning on the way to work. But you will remember the Lamborghini.

You saw something out of the ordinary, remembered it, and told someone else about it. It got *into your head.* In a nutshell, you did what every publicist goes to bed at night hoping you'll do.

I first realized the power of being remembered (for good or for bad) back in junior high school. I went to junior high on Staten Island, a suburb 20 minutes outside of New York City. If Staten Island had a motto for kids, it would have been "Staten Island: Where being different is wrong." The kids in Junior High School 61 were not really fond of being different—you either fit the mold of what was cool or you were an outcast, destined to spend your sixth, seventh, and eighth grade years in social-misfit land with the other geeks, dorks, and those who didn't belong.

Rather than come home crying every day (which I did a lot, don't get me wrong), I figured out at an early age that it wouldn't be such a bad thing to embrace the differences and learn to capitalize on them. I figured I had two choices: be attacked for my differences, or use them to my advantage. If I did the former, I'd continue to be miserable. If I did the latter, perhaps I could change things. If the latter didn't work, I'd just get beaten up some more—no real loss. But perhaps I could become known for something more than just being an outsider and maybe even turn my daily beat-up sessions into something more productive.

I was born with a learning disability. A "motor-visual impairment," they called it. Basically, I read and processed things a heck of a lot faster than I could write them. This caused issues in class, because I'd read what was on the board, process it, then get totally frustrated when I couldn't write it down. Some smart doctor somewhere suggested I take a portable word processor to class. This was in the early 1980s–a portable computer still weighed close to ten pounds, but had (get this!) 2k of RAM. Two whole kilobytes! Woo!

Anyhow, try taking your notes in class on a portable word processor when you're *already* not too well liked. Didn't go over too well, and my daily beat-up sessions increased.

But then one day, as I was rubbing out a bruise to my ribs, it occurred to me–I was typing my notes so fast that I had tons of time left. All the other kids were still writing, and hating it. So what if I offered to help them?

Peter's Note-Taking-Service was born. I didn't charge anyone, I just told one or two of the more influential kids (influencer beings–we'll talk about them later) that hey, if you needed today's English or History notes, just let me know–I could print off a page from the word processor's memory.

The beatings slowed down a bit. I became useful. I was still a dork, an outsider, but I was a dork with a purpose. Word spread, and soon enough, I was printing out class notes for some of the most popular kids, the meanest kids, and even one or two other outcasts like me.

That too, was a form of PR. Much like a client who has no news, I didn't (at the time) have much going for me. I wasn't cool, or hot, or good-looking, or popular. I didn't have news. But I had a portable word processor. That made me stand out in a way not one other classmate could. I was able to get people to see the positive possibilities in difference, and that led to an attitude change, a shift. I began to be treated differently, and it made the final year of junior high just a little less terrible.

I used a difference–in this case, my disability–to my advantage. This was the first of hundreds of times I'd turn a disability or problem into an ability or solution over the course of my personal and professional life.

It occurred to me right then that if you just look at things a little differently, the whole game changes. I wasn't the dork with the typewriter, I was a valuable tool for the cool kids. I wasn't another Honda Civic to be ignored on the highway of life, I was a fire-engine-red Lamborghini, zooming into your memory.

Learning to understand how to make something different, or something nontraditional, or even the lack of something (new news, for instance) work to your advantage can put you light years ahead of your competition.

Fast forward to high school. Doing much better now, I'd found a school where everyone was a bit odd—thus, we were all ok together. Of course, that made it a lot harder to stand out. How do you stand out in a room full of freaks when you've learned to use your freak-ness to stand out in the first place?

And how do you pitch your company when several companies like yours are doing exactly the same thing?

You adapt. You find something they're not doing, you do that, and you tell the world all about it.

I went to a school with a really, really, expensive concert hall and theater. We were a performing arts school, so it only made sense. Problem was, there weren't enough people to run it.

Like any school, mine relied on students to pick up most of the grunt-work slack. And what kid wants to do grunt-work on a gorgeous after-school day in April, when the Sheep Meadow in Central Park is calling to you?

You do, if you know what it can get you.

Most people think in terms of what I call "immediate gimmie." That is, if I do X right now, what's the immediate result? Too many people don't think five minutes ahead of the "right now," let alone five days, weeks, or months. In the PR world, which seems on the surface to operate by that same principle of instant gratification, the opposite is in fact true: thinking just a little bit ahead, asking, "Well, what can we get out of this next week? Next month? Next year?" can give you that edge when you're offering a reporter a tidbit of new information.

What happens if a reporter knows that you're always available and your clients are happy to help whenever he needs something? He's going to call you first. Why would he know to do this? Because you thought ahead, and in September, sent him an email that said, "Hey, when you're swamped in a few months, call me—I'll be around to help."

Think ahead.

For me, asking, "Well, what can I get out of working in the concert hall on this gorgeous day?" got me more than I ever imagined. It got me the golden keys to the school, as it were. I was able to go anywhere, do anything, miss class, hand in work according to my schedule, all because I was working in the concert hall. I became known as the guy with the keys to the school. And it was an accurate description. My giving up that gorgeous after-school time in the park got me tons of connections that came in very handy as I went through my days at LaGuardia High School of Performing Arts.

Remember: There'll always be another sunny day in the park, but there might be only one time to get in the good graces of a reporter, or one time to come up with the idea or event that separates you from the masses. Do that right, and you can spend as much time in the park as you want—you'll be brilliant. And brilliant people get to do whatever they want.

How's That Latte? Almost Gone?

So you're still sipping that latte, on the floor of the bookstore. Well, you now have some idea of how I think—and you'll soon learn why I think it's in your best interest to throw reporters out of a plane, or flood a city street with a soft drink. So how do you do it? How do you convince the bosses? How do you convince the board? How do you do it on the cheap? How do you make the media care? How do you create a return on investment?

In the end, it's surprisingly simple. You probably already know what to do, you've just never thought of the rules quite that way before. One of the greatest aspects of event and stunt driven

PR I've found, over and over again, is that the best ideas are the simplest ones. The ideas that make reporters, producers, editors, and the public stand up and take notice are the ones that you come up with and everyone else goes, "Why didn't I think of that?" They're the ideas that change someone's most basic way of thinking. Not because you've solved the unsolvable scientific equation, but because you've made someone think in a different way. By subtly altering another person's perception, you've made them think in a way they never before thought possible.

You can learn to do that over and over again, for client after client, company after company, news event after news event. You can learn to do it in such a way that you're not being repetitive, you're not being boring, people don't think of you as a one-trick pony. You can grow your ideas and your company, just by altering your perception a little bit.

So throw the latte cup away (it's probably cold by now, anyway), buy this book, and start reading. The public won't know what hit them.

?!

CHAPTER 2

PR Basics

I'm going to devote one or two pages to the PR Fundamentals. These aren't the PR Basics, which will comprise the rest of this chapter. The PR Fundamentals are even more basic than the PR Basics! The Fundamentals give you the ten-second cocktail party overview of what Public Relations is.

A beautiful woman walks into a bar. You see her, and go over to her. You tell her, "I'm spectacular in bed; you should really come home with me." That's advertising. Chances are, she won't believe you and most likely, you'll get a drink thrown in your face for your trouble. Why should someone take anything you say about yourself with anything less than several grains of salt?

So let's try again.

A beautiful woman walks into a bar. You see her, and you're mesmerized. But instead of going over to her and telling her how great you are in bed, her best friend, also in the bar, does it for you. She goes over and says, "You know, that guy over there, the one who's checking you out, I've heard about him. He's amazing in bed. He runs his own company, drives a Porsche, has a cat, and is nice to his mother. He's an all-around perfect guy. You should really go over and talk to him." As she's finishing her little speech about why you're so perfect, another friend goes over to her and says, "You and that guy would be totally perfect for each other. He's so sweet!" And so on, and so on.

Finally, she comes over to you; "I hear you and I have a lot in common. Buy me a drink."

That, in a nutshell is fundamental public relations. You've created a basic story. Somehow, through good chatter, a well-positioned message, a good story, you've crafted a message that has gotten out to the masses. It's been heard and retold by other people; it's been given credibility.

You can tell your story in a number of ways, if you're a company. You can issue a press release. You can take a reporter to lunch and tell him or her in person. You can hold a press conference. You can create a wild and wacky stunt. There are many ways to get your message out. Which one works for you? It all depends on the message you're trying to get across.

Has the company stock taken a massive tumble after top management was caught stealing funds? Probably not a good time to create a wacky stunt. But launching a new soft drink? Take the hottest day of the year, and fill an Olympic-sized swimming pool with it. If it's carbonated, all the better. Invite the world over to swim with the bubbles.

Quintessentially, good PR is taking some kind of story, either good or bad, putting your specific angle or "spin" (although I hate that word) on it, and then convincing reporters, editors, producers, and the public, to talk about it.

That's it! Go forth and prosper.

So why does it feel like it's so damn hard to do?

Because hundreds of thousands of companies are trying to do it every single day, and there just isn't enough interest to go around. So the media (and as a result, the public) has to be picky as to what they find interesting, and from whom they want to hear more.

So your job is not only to craft a good story and pitch it to the right people, but also to do it in such a way that you make people want to hear more. In fact, you'll know you're doing your job well when people ask *you* for more information, rather than you having to go and force it on them.

GOOD PR VERSUS BAD PR VERSUS NO PR

Five (true) examples of bad press releases that got absolutely no attention, whatsoever:

1. Acme Company moves to higher floor in same building
2. President of Acme Company to give speech
3. Acme Company Allows "Office-Wide Hawaiian Shirt Day, every other Summer Friday"
4. Acme Company launches new product
5. Acme Company hires new VP

Hey! Wake up! You just nodded off!

I know. Those were painful, weren't they? But why?

Well, let's look at them. While moving to a higher floor might be a wonderful accomplishment (Hey, we've outgrown our office and hired four new people; we're going from the 5th floor to the 8th!) who, outside your office, would possibly care?

Your CEO is giving a speech. Unless he's Bill Gates or Richard Branson, and about to launch a brand new product that will appeal to at least 97 percent of the world, don't bother sending this kind of release to more than the few editors who already know you. Don't waste your time (or electrons, or the reporter's time) by sending it out widely.

Hawaiian Shirt Day. Do I really need to say more? The frightening thing is, this was an actual release, issued by a real, live company in 2002. They thought it would make them look cool. Trust me. It didn't. Man oh man, how it didn't.

You're launching a new product. This actually could be some news. But not presented like that. Again—who's your audience? Where is the release going? What's the product? Why is it different? Sadly, too many people get so involved in the day-to-day, they forget that people outside their walls have no idea about the product and need to be educated.

Finally, the classic "new hire" release. This has some merit, if done well. If not, it hits the trash before it's even opened.

There are many ways to recognize bad PR. Not unlike a bad date, bad PR gives off warning signs. Following are a few of the most common, along with the crucial "what-not-to-do" rules they illustrate.

The "No news" warning sign: This is a dead giveaway, and the most obvious of the no-nos. You're moving up four flights to your new office. To put it bluntly, NO ONE CARES. If you were leasing the entire building, yes—it would matter. You're switching offices. It's not important.

?!?!?!?!?!?!?!?

> **Rule: If it's not important, it's not worth talking about.**

The "Doing it to kiss the CEO's butt" warning sign: Do you really want to put out a press release that the CEO is speaking to the local senior citizens' center? Will that really bring the media? Highly doubtful. What it will do, though, is cost you time, money, and effort, not to mention forcing you to deal with the CEO's wrath when no media shows up anyway, as you predicted.

?!?!?!?!?!?!?!?

> **Rule: If the CEO wants his butt kissed, find a nonpublic way to do it.**

The "Am I the only person who realizes how damn STUPID this makes us look?" warning sign: Sometimes clients, or people in management, do certain things (because they think it'll result in an increased coolness factor) when in actuality, it does exactly the opposite—it moves the needle on the Dork-o-Meter off the charts. This is delicate, because it's up to you to teach the clueless how horribly bad their idea really is.

?!?!?!?!?!?!?!?

> **Rule: If you cringe while reading it and want to hide your face, the media will pity you. And pity will NOT get you positive press.**

The "New product! Check it out, I've got a new product here,"
warning sign: This one is tricky, because it hides itself. Everyone is so excited about the new product that you forget that (1)
not everyone is aware of it and you *are* indeed going to need to
explain, and (2) you haven't re-invented Pi. While it may be the
most important thing to hit your company in the past 20 years,
for the rest of the world, it's Tuesday.

?!?!?!?!?!?!?!?

Rule: A new product, on its own, does not guarantee press. It never will.

The "Tad Johnson has just started working here" warning sign:
Fortunately, this warning sign has a great and easy litmus test:
Go ask three people in your industry who don't know that good
old Tad is joining your company if they know who good old Tad
is to begin with. If two of the three do not, then mentioning Tad's
name will *not* get you a table at Spago. You can still issue this release, but you'll want to adhere to certain rules, the least of
which is the "Because you're not Bill Clinton, that's why," rule.

?!?!?!?!?!?!?!?

Rule: If you're not famous, simply putting your name in the title of the release will not get you media attention.

SO WHAT DO WE DO?

Reporters get, on average, upwards of 200 emails a day. How
many do you think they really look at?

Much like that statistic that says hiring managers look at resumes and make a decision in less than six seconds, so do reporters when it comes to wanting to find out more. Think about
it for a second: each email a reporter gets asks for, at the very
least, his or her time. *Please use your valuable time to cover my*

story. But a reporter only has so much valuable time. In fact, with deadlines the way they are in today's 24-hour-news-on-demand world, reporters have less time than ever.

Ask any public relations professional over 50, and he or she will tell you—it used to be a lot easier. You wrote a press release when you had real news. You sent it to reporters, via mail (regular mail!). That meant you typed it up (on a typewriter!) put it in an envelope, addressed and stamped the envelope, and then dropped it in the mailbox. (Amazing!)

But that's what you did. And the reporter would get it, and read it, and either print it straight, or get back to you with questions.

Then faxes came along. Then email. Now, any idiot with an idea can buy a list and send out a press release to 10,000 journalists in 14 seconds, the majority who have absolutely no interest *whatsoever* in your so-called news. Multiply each piece of "news" by several follow-up emails saying, "Hi, just checking in, did you get my really important news?" and you can kind of start to figure out how the love-hate relationship between journalists and public relations people got started.

To compound the problem, too many students are graduating with degrees in Public Relations, and start working for their first employer with the horrible assumption that "pitch to the masses, follow up, follow up, follow up" is the best, most effective way to do PR. And they're wrong.

Nowadays, more reporters are turning away blind pitches within four seconds of receiving the email. The subject line will determine whether an email gets opened, and the opening line determines whether the email gets read. This isn't a steadfast rule to which every reporter adheres, but I can tell you, more and more reporters simply don't want to waste their time reading pitches that continue to be off target, not what they cover, or simply put, bad.

But wait! You're reading this book! That means that you've already realized that writing crappy pitches, wasting reporters' time, and emailing or calling multiple times just doesn't work!

You know this because you're just a trifle smarter than everyone else. That trifle is all you need.

IN PR, AS IN LIFE, TAKE ADVANTAGE OF OTHER PEOPLE'S STUPIDITY

Let's say you're 5 feet 10 inches tall, and weigh about 195 pounds. Unless all of that is muscle, you probably have a little bit of flab on you. Maybe your stomach isn't completely flat, maybe you have a double-butt or a "muffin top" that you just can't get rid of.

When you're out in public and want to make sure you look your best and get noticed, with whom do you go out? With your drop-dead-gorgeous, abs-of-steel best friend, who runs Triathlons in her sleep for fun, or your other friend, the one who's 5 feet 7 inches and 190? You know the answer.

You're not being mean, you're simply taking advantage of a situation. Same thing when you're checking in for a flight. Get in line behind the idiot yelling at the gate agent, and be as nice and cooperative as possible–your chances of an upgrade just went through the stratosphere.

By counting on other people's stupidity, and showing just a hint of intelligence, you've already jumped ahead of 95 percent of all the other email Mr. Reporter got today. You don't have an exclusive on anything. You don't have the hottest news in the world. Yet your email gets opened, read, and acted on. Why?

Because, as I said above, the majority of PR people don't know the most basic rules. The rules of the PR game, which are very much like the rules of life, are not hard to figure out, once you learn them. Write this down–there will be a quiz later.

A Publicist's Rules for Life (and for PR)

1. Your goal is to make other people happy (the reporter, for instance). Do this, and you, the boss, and the client will be happy by default.

2. We have a finite number of seconds on this earth. Don't waste them. Get to the point, be direct, and get your information out there. Don't waste time.
3. Don't be traditional. If you have something to say, find an interesting way to say it. If you can't, it's probably not worth saying in the first place.
4. Don't bore people. Boring turns people against you. Nothing makes someone put a block on your email quicker than a pointless email, and nothing causes someone to not want to talk to you again quicker than being boring and repetitive.
5. Have fun, and help someone out when you can. Karma is strong, especially in PR, an industry where you have nothing until a reporter, editor, or producer gives you something.

To understand this concept a bit better, let's take our five headlines again, and reread them. Perhaps we'll even change them around a little bit.

Horrible Headlines That Got No Action Whatsoever

1. Acme Company moves to higher floor in same building
2. President of Acme Company to give speech
3. Acme Company Allows "Office-Wide Hawaiian Shirt Day, every other Summer Friday"
4. Acme Company launches new product
5. Acme Company hires new VP

We've already talked about why they're not getting any attention. No one cares about your move from the 5th floor to the 8th floor. It's not newsworthy.

Or is it?

Let's think about it for a second. You're moving from one floor to another. Obviously, you need more space because you've expanded. Your company is growing. Ok . . . so how about:

ACME COMPANY DOUBLES IN SIZE IN TWO YEARS, SIGNS MULTI-YEAR DEAL ON NEW SPACE

That's a little better, right? Shows a little more insight into the company, makes it a little bit more newsworthy. You've taken two stories and made them if not compelling, then at least a little more than a snooze-fest. But can we improve? Me thinks so:

ACME COMPANY, REPORTING RECORD GROWTH, ANNOUNCES DOUBLING IN SIZE IN 24 MONTHS, PROFITS AT HIGHEST POINT EVER—SIGNS MULTI-YEAR DEAL ON NEW S PACE

Ok, now we're getting somewhere! This is actual news! We like this! A reporter, one who covers the space in which Acme Company lives, might actually find this interesting! All of a sudden, Acme Company is a player! "They're obviously doing something right," thinks the reporter, "look at how much they've grown!"

Let's back up a second. What if you don't have record profits? Perhaps you're doing ok, growing, getting a bigger office, but you haven't doubled. You've added employees, and you're steadily increasing your revenues. All of a sudden, we've gone from "Hmm, this could be interesting," back to "Well, call me when you have some real news."

So it might be time to look at other angles. What else can you do to get some coverage? You're still moving to a different floor—that's going to happen whether the media reports on you or not. And you're still growing. Ok, good. What else can you use as a hook?

How about *thinking differently*? Are you a local business? Are you involved in your community? Since you're moving, what about "giving back" to the community, and hiring the less fortunate to help you move? What good (and newsworthy) community residents you would be if you offered those at the local shelter or halfway house a job for the day? You'd be giving back to your community, you'd be helping people get back on their feet, you'd probably even save some money and, oh yeah, you'd be taking a boring "we're moving upstairs" story and turning it into a spectacular, newsworthy, "good news/feel good" local story, which would be sure to generate some press, as well as a lot of goodwill.

So how about that headline now?

ACME COMPANY OFFERS A "DAY OF THANKS" TO LOCAL
COMMUNITY FOR RECORD GROWTH AND PROFITS
SIGNS MULTI-YEAR DEAL ON NEW SPACE, AND WILL GIVE BACK
TO CENTERVILLE'S LESS FORTUNATE ON MARCH 15TH

What has this headline done? It's not only made a business story interesting (Hey, they had record growth and profits? Let's talk to them!) but it's also opened the story up to the local community reporters—and if you're in a small town, they're much more important than the business press anyhow. Everyone reads page 1, but only a quarter of the people open up to the business section.

There you go. You're employing the Five Rules. They're working for you. Look at what we did: We went from:

ACME COMPANY MOVES TO HIGHER FLOOR IN SAME BUILDING

to:

ACME COMPANY OFFERS A "DAY OF THANKS" TO LOCAL
COMMUNITY FOR RECORD GROWTH AND PROFITS—SIGNS
MULTI-YEAR DEAL ON NEW SPACE, AND WILL GIVE BACK TO
CENTERVILLE'S LESS FORTUNATE ON MARCH 15TH

Nice, huh? Just a little creativity, and a different way of thinking.

Let's do one more.

PRESIDENT OF ACME COMPANY TO GIVE SPEECH

Wow, that email will go in the recycle bin so fast, it'll make your spleen hurt. That's just not good.

So what can we do to fix it? What are our choices?

First of all, what's your president talking about? To whom is he saying it? What's the subject? Is it about the company, or has he been asked to speak somewhere about something else? If the former, what media would be interested? And if the latter, who invited him, and why did they invite him, as opposed to anyone else? These are the types of questions you should always be asking yourself because you're thinking differently about everything now.

So let's say the local business council asked your president to speak. Ok. That's a start, right?

LOCAL BUSINESS COUNCIL INVITES ACME COMPANY

CEO TO KEYNOTE BUSINESS LUNCHEON

In that one brief change, you've made your CEO, the speech itself, and where he's speaking a lot stronger. You *could* stop there, but you're not traditional. You think differently now.

Ask yourself: Who attends these business luncheons? Why do they go? Well, people attend them to learn, to network with their peers, to eat. . . . Ok. Let's take that somewhere, and see where we wind up.

ACME COMPANY CEO TO KEYNOTE BUSINESS

NETWORKING LUNCH OF TOP CENTERVILLE EXECUTIVES

Better! Now it's looking good, and might get a line or two in the calendar column. Let's see, though, if we can't give it one more kick in the pants. Let's tie it into something relevant in today's world. That way, it becomes *timely*. It's not just about your CEO speaking, but about real-world issues affecting all of us right now. And remember, the concept of "right now" and "affecting all of us" is massive. You can turn a lot of heads and build a lot of story if you tie it into time and effect.

ACME COMPANY CEO TO KEYNOTE CENTERVILLE'S LARGEST

BUSINESS NETWORKING EVENT TO DISCUSS HOW WORLD

FINANCIAL ISSUES ARE AFFECTING CENTERVILLE AND

OUR LOCAL ECONOMY

Bingo. I'd go listen to him speak. I bet the media would, too.

GETTING THE MEDIA TO LOVE YOU

I remember a friend once called me, furious that the reporter didn't mention him in a second story he did on my friend's industry.

"Why should he have mentioned you?" I asked my friend.

"Because after he didn't mention my company in the first story, I called him up and ripped him a new one! I told him that he should be ashamed of himself and not even call himself a journalist if he didn't do his basic homework to realize that my company is in the space he covered!"

I just silently shook my head.

"And then he had the nerve to not mention us AGAIN, in the second story he did!"

"Yes, what a shock, I'm floored," I deadpanned.

Ok, you were smart enough to buy this book, so you're smart enough to see where I'm going with this. Please tell me that I don't have to explain to you why my friend didn't get any coverage, and why I was shaking my head in exasperated pity. Mind you, I'd be willing to bet that my friend has never been upgraded to first class at the airport either.

What good could my friend have possibly thought would come from telling a reporter off? Who had the complete upper hand here? I'd say the reporter—after all, the reporter chose not to mention his company. The reporter determined who was going to be featured in the story, and who wasn't.

Imagine you want to pet a dog for the first time. You put your hand out, and it runs across the room. Which next step would give you a better shot at petting the dog?

a. Slowly putting your hand out, calling to the dog in a soft voice, and showing it that you're not a threat.
b. Running to the dog while screaming, "I'LL PET YOU IF I WANT TO PET YOU, YOU STUPID DOG! DON'T YOU KNOW WHO I AM? HOW DARE YOU NOT WANT TO BE PETTED BY SOMEONE AS GREAT OF A PETTER AS ME?!"

You get the idea. Well sure enough, my friend chose tactic b and lived to regret it. That reporter—someone who could have been key in advancing his career—has NEVER covered his company.

In general, reporters, editors, producers, even assignment desk clerks–they all have the upper hand. We want something from them. We want coverage, a story, a two-minute national piece. Whatever it is, we want it from them, and they have the power to give it to us–or not.

These are the people who can turn us into heroes overnight. These are the members of the human race who, with one decision, one flick of a switch, one flourish of a pen, can turn unknown companies into worldwide household names.

They can also make sure our most brilliant idea never sees the light of day. Ever.

I'd say it's in your best interest to be nice to them. And not only because you want something from them right now. But always. Because hey . . . you never know.

?!?!?!?!?!?!?!?

Rule: Whatever you think your job is, it isn't. This is your job: Treat people (reporters, editors, dogs) well. They'll remember. Be respectful to them; teach them that even if you disagree, you'll be courteous and good to work with. Teach them that you'll be there for them for whatever they need, when they need it, and you'll help them do whatever it takes to make their life easier. That's your job.

Corollary to this rule: If you're an idiot and call the reporter out, thinking you'll be the bad-ass, you'll wind up getting smacked around so hard you won't remember your name. This will happen every single time. If you work for a company, you can be assured that the company won't ever be covered. If you work for an agency and you call the reporter out, there's a possibility that you've also doomed every client that agency has. And that . . . well, that's just not good for you.

Addendum to that rule: It's even more fun to put that rule into practice when the person right before you played the corollary. It makes you look like a hero.

So . . . we're learning to be nice.

Let's talk about some other basics that will instantly turn you into a PR pariah.

We know how busy reporters are. Yet countless times each day, reporters get hit with information about which they honestly could not care less. Why? It's simple.

The process happens like this: A boss, or a client, calls you in and says "This release has to go out today. Make sure you hit at least 50 editors. And follow up!"

You agree (not because you don't know any better, but because hey, he's the boss, and you like getting a paycheck) and you go and sit down at your desk. "OK. I need 50 outlets for this. Where do I start? I don't know 50 journalists who would want this pitch! I don't know three. This pitch is tailored to a specific market and a specific audience. There aren't 50 reporters in the world who would cover this, let alone in my city/state/country."

So you do a search in one of the online sourcebooks, which yields a tremendously helpful two sources. You then Google the topic, which gives you one. You've got three. You need 50. By 5:30 P.M.

So you go into Lexis-Nexis, and do a search on your key word. You pull four names. Where are you going to get the other 43 names?

Easy. You'll do a search on a much broader category–"Tech," for instance. Or maybe "Breathing," as in, "a reporter who is . . ."

You get your 50. You send out the release.

Then, you sit there dumbfounded the next morning when you're back to the crickets and tumbleweeds, occasionally interrupted by the email of an editor saying, "I don't cover this; you didn't do any homework; don't waste my time and don't email me again."

Well done.

Imagine if you worked for a Chinese take-out restaurant, and you were in charge of answering the phones and taking the orders. You'd be busy all the time making sure the orders were right, the delivery addresses were correct, you'd be under constant pressure, from the moment you walked in until the moment you left.

Now add to that the following scenario: Every third phone call is from someone asking to order a pizza. Or perhaps wanting information about a new car purchase. Or maybe looking to book a flight to Los Angeles.

Would kinda drive you crazy, huh?

Unfortunately, that's what reporters deal with from clueless PR professionals on a daily basis. They get email after email, dealing with exactly what they DON'T cover. Why would they give you the time of day? If they're really nice and not too swamped, they'll email you telling exactly how much of an idiot you really are, and exactly how you should go about never, ever contacting them again.

If they *are* swamped, they'll just add you to their kill-file and with one stroke, make sure you're never heard from again. If you're really annoying, they'll make sure your company or agency as a whole is never heard from again.

Let us also not forget what happens when you put emails out there—they become public. With more and more websites and blogs being started by journalists, it's not uncommon to see your horrible pitch on a "bad pitch" blog, made fun of by the masses for eternity.

That's not the kind of press you want. However, in a "learning from other people's mistakes" kind of way, and not in a "ha-ha, sucks to be you" kind of way, I've included a few of these sites in the Resources section at the back of the book. Study and learn. Don't be a statistic.

When I find a reporter I've never met before who I think would be interested in one of my clients, I drop him an email, introducing myself. Not a pitch, not a "Hey! Cover my client!" email, just a quick note, letting them know that I enjoyed their last story, and if they're doing another one at any point, they're welcome to give me a call and I'll gladly put them in touch with my client. That's all. The email takes maybe 10 seconds to read and lets the reporter know he has a source when he needs it.

The reporter can file the source, and move on. Takes 30 seconds out of my day, 10 seconds out of his, but helps us both.

Obviously, the key to finding these reporters is research. You should be reading everything. When you find a reporter you want to learn more about, set up a free Google News Alert: http://news.google.com will get you started. I must have a hundred or so of these on different clients, topics, reporters, heck, even potential clients. Create a throw-away email address for these alerts, and check it once a day. When someone's name gets picked up by a Google alert, I get notified immediately, and it's the easiest thing in the world to drop a quick email—"Hey, I saw your article on XYZ. Well done!" or, "Hey, I saw your company got mentioned in the story about XYZ. Congratulations!"

It's showing you're interested, showing you won't waste time, and showing you care that will grow your profile with the media, keep you above the fold, as it were, and allow you to get those stories and placements that seemed so elusive in the past.

Finally, let's talk about a good karma email. A good karma email is exactly what it sounds like: an email designed to offer a little bit of help to a reporter, or ease his or her burden at five minutes to deadline.

Once a year, I send out these good karma emails to thousands of reporters. They don't ask for *anything*. This is an important aspect of the email, one that I can't stress enough. I am not spamming thousands of reporters asking for coverage. Go back and reread that last line a few hundred times until it sticks in your brain. I am NOT spamming thousands of reporters and asking them for coverage. Spam sucks. I will never do it. Ever.

What I *am* doing, though, is offering my help. Offering my vast list of contacts. Offering my expertise. Perhaps one day they'll write a story about adventure sports—well, I'm a licensed skydiver. They just might turn to me to give them some quotes or data.

Or maybe one day they'll be reassigned to a desk where they need to build up their contacts. Maybe they'll call me at that point and ask if I can help.

Maybe they'll even be doing a story on an industry in which my client is a leader, and remember that I represent them, call me, and get my client into the story.

Who knows? Regardless of the outcome, I'm doing it for the karma points.

The following email was sent out in January of 2006, to approximately 4,000 reporters around the world.

!?!

Dear Jonathan,

Consider this a PR guy's attempt at good karma for a Sunday afternoon, when it's snowing, and quite frankly, just too cold to go outside into the freezing depths of Manhattan. So I'm sitting on my couch with my two psychotic cats (http://www.geekfactory.com/geekcats.htm) and figured it was a good time to do my yearly "PR Karma."

First off, this is SO not a pitch. Quite the opposite—this is an offer of help. I do this about once a year—the media seem to like it.

In a nutshell, I'm inviting you to source me. Add me to your email list when you're desperately seeking a quote at 11 minutes to deadline. Call me when something major breaks. Put me in your Rolodex, and feel free to dial.

And no, this is not to get me in the press.

Basically, I just know a LOT of people. Between the amount of time I travel for business (in excess of 200k miles a year), the number of advisory boards on which I sit, the amount of clients I have, and the fact that I'm just a talkative (some might say hyperactive), nice, total ADHD guy who only sleeps about four hours a night to begin with, I have a Palm Pilot bursting at the seams.

This isn't about my clients, by the way. In fact, they're the smallest category. Mostly it's people I've become friends/colleagues with in some capacity, who do the most random things. Identity theft investigators. Litigators who only work on animal-related lawsuits. The guy who manufactures the laces that go in 75 percent of the world's sneakers . . . Knitters who only knit with soy, bamboo, or hemp yarn. The Director of Arts Education for the NYC Department of Education. A director of security for a large nationwide upscale department store. A child psychologist who only works with high risk, suicidal kids. A guy with over 5,000 skydives under his belt. A former Navy SEAL who now teaches mortals like me how to stay in shape. The guy who designs solar clothing that lights up with messages on the back. All friends, people I've met on airplanes or while jumping out of them, who I met at Sushi dinners, talked to while running marathons, or swimming the Escape From Alcatraz Triathlon (which was, as expected, REALLY cold).

Really RANDOM people—I happen to know them. Mostly because I do really random things.

I also have some great clients—Dream Catcher Retreats, AirTroductions, OpSec Security, and a bunch of others. In addition, I throw a good number of events and parties during the year, and am constantly looking for members of the media who would enjoy attending. If that's you, let me know, as well. See, I don't sleep much.

So like I said, consider it good Karma. I run a PR shop in New York City called The Geek Factory, Inc. (Seriously—www.geekfactory.com). If I'm able to offer you a source that winds up helping you get in under a deadline, or makes a story more colorful, then cool. If it helps a client, great, but if it doesn't, like I said, it's all about Karma. Who knows where it will lead?

Anyhow, source me. That's my offer for this afternoon. My contact information is below. Add me to whatever rolodex you're currently using, and if I can help in any way, feel free to call.

All the best,

Peter Shankman
CEO
The Geek Factory, Inc.

P.S.: Don't worry—this isn't a list from which you need to be removed. I won't start sending out weekly updates or anything, I promise. And to answer the second most frequently asked question, I got your name from Media Map, the PR/Journalist tool.

!?!

And that's it. I include all my phone numbers (mobile, home, office, etc.) and an alternate email. (Deadlines don't respect voice mail.)

Last year's email resulted in a response rate of around 50 percent, and I'm still helping these reporters out on a regular basis. I've even become friends with some of them.

I've had a reporter who have called me asking if I knew if restaurants had any plans to do anything special with potatoes this year. (I knew a chef, I put the two of them together.) Another reporter called me and asked me about craft fairs. (How fortunate for me that one of my clients sells yarn!)

The real coup, for me, was a local reporter in New York asking if I knew anyone worthy of a feature article–nonfamous people. Three weeks later, my mom and dad had their smiling faces plastered in the *Daily News.*

Why did I get all this press for my clients, my friends (my parents!), and random people I only met once? As I said before, good karma. It helps. It makes the reporter happy. It makes the client happy. It makes the random person you've only met once happy. But it's a good thing to do. It'll come back to help you.

I can't tell you how many clients I've gotten through word of mouth. Come to think of it, yes, I can: all of them. We've never advertised. We've never done anything remotely close to advertising.

But our name gets out there. Reporters get asked all the time by potential PR clients, "So, you know anyone in the PR space? We want to hire an agency." I get over half my clients that way.

Reporters are your friends. They want to be! While they're rarely going to admit this, the fact is, for as much as we can't live without them, they can't live without us, either. Reporters need us to bring them stories. They need us to get them quotes from executives, and they need us to remind those executives when the interview is.

Of course, take that above paragraph, but don't get cocky with it. Reporters still have the control over what they write. And they can still smack you when they feel like it.

A delicate balance, this PR game is. But oh, so much fun to play.

WHAT WE LEARNED
FROM THIS CHAPTER

1. Thinking differently—this is of major importance. Normal people tend to get treated normally. Mostly though, they get ignored. Be a bit above normal, you'll get some good attention.

2. Reporters are our friends. They need to be. But: **WE DO NOT CONTROL THEM.** We can't control what they write, we can't delude ourselves into thinking we can. It doesn't work that way. We can, however, suggest, offer, and support. This will help us, will help our clients, and our business. But we do not control what they write. The second we start to think we do, we'll be smacked down so fast, our heads will spin.

3. Learn to craft a press release that doesn't put people to sleep. Your CEO can tell you something that will put you to sleep. Your amazing craft of a job is to turn the snoozer into something caffeinated. Think about the release. What can you do differently to it? What can you do that grows it, that takes it to a level where someone won't immediately delete it? Can you add another level of creativity to it? A local level? What can you do that adds some kind of *hook* to it? Something that not only keeps the reporters' eyes open, but makes them go, "OK, cool. I can write about that."

4. Remember what a reporter covers, and hit that reporter with what he covers. DON'T hit the reporter with what he doesn't cover. The reporter will hit back. Don't "mass-blast." You'll get virtually no coverage, and lose a lot of future chances for coverage.

5. Finally, know your reporters before you pitch them. Regardless of what you're doing—a stunt, a typical release, anything—know the reporter. Know the likes and dislikes of the reporter before you go to them with a release. They might like only a paragraph. Or just key points with nothing else. KNOW first. Then go.

6. Super-finally: have fun. I'll say this over and over again. Have fun. PR is a fun game. You can really enjoy yourself, if you do it right. So do it right. Have fun.

CHAPTER 3

Coming Up with the Off-the-Wall Idea, and Making It Stick

This chapter will focus on how to train your brain to:

- Come up with the big idea,
- Suggest the big idea,
- Not fear the response, and
- Get it approved!

In the doorway of my office, dead center to the top, and extremely visible to any visitor is a sign. It reads: **SUGGEST ANYTHING.**

Pretty self-explanatory, I think. Yet, I can count on more than two hands the number of times my employees dismissed an idea without even bringing it up for debate because they just assumed, "Oh, he won't like it."

If you dismiss an idea outright, you're guaranteeing yourself one thing only: Your idea will never see the light of day. No matter how good it is, no matter how many people can improve on it, and no matter how many suggestions will make it the next "Pet Rock," you're guaranteeing that it will never even get close to that kind of recognition.

Why would you want to do that, not only to yourself, but to your wonderful idea? Imagine if Alexander Graham Bell had said, "Oh, I can't get this thing to work. I won't bother finishing it. No one is going to want to talk to people over wires by holding something up to their ear, anyway."

Never kill your ideas, no matter how weird or "out-there" they might sound. Believe me—over the course of your life in PR, there'll be enough people in the world ready to kill your ideas. You should *never be one of them.*

We'll get more into the art of *defending your idea* a little later in this chapter. However, before we can defend your great new idea, you have to come up with one. And if you're sitting in a cube farm all day, day after day, you're probably not going to come up with that many off-the-wall ideas.

How many times have you heard someone (usually someone who doesn't work in PR) talk about what you do for a living, and say, "Oh, I could never be that creative. I don't know how you're so creative. Wow. You're just . . . so creative!"

One of my skydiving buddies said that to me once. We were talking about a new idea I had for a t-shirt and she laughed and said, "It's good the world has people like you—you're just so creative. It makes it fun for the rest of us." I accepted the compliment and was flattered, then I thought about her for a second.

When she's not hurling herself out of a plane at 120 miles per hour, she's an administrator in the drama department in a major university. She's constantly asked by the students in her department to be in plays, films, and the like. She's a classically trained actress, and she's modeled professionally. She's also a yoga instructor.

And she's telling me that she's not creative?

I would argue that the only reason she thinks she's not creative, is because *she thinks she's not creative!* I would say that, given all the different outlets she has for her energy (acting, photography, skydiving, yoga) that she's one of the most creative people I know! Yet she doesn't see it that way.

Hence . . . the only "How to be creative Rule" there is:

We're all born creative. All you need to do is allow yourself to be creative.

The great baseball player, Satchel Paige, was fond of saying, "How old would you be if you didn't know how old you are?"

Think about it. For some reason, we're controlled by our ages. We shouldn't be, but we are. It's probably because we're a numbers society. We like the *finiteness of a number*. We like being able to measure. But we weren't always like that.

When you're a kid, and I mean a really young kid, you are controlled by one aspect of your life: your imagination. Go to the park on a Saturday and watch the kids playing. Borrow a niece or nephew, and take the kid to the playground. See how he or she plays in the sandbox, or runs around with that high-pitched "EEEE!" scream that only young kids without a care in the world can make. It's not about deadlines or meetings, or doing what's expected. Children play because they don't have restrictions on their imaginations.

Where exactly is it written that when we grow up and become "adults" in "the real world," we're not allowed to have an imagination anymore?

A friend of mine, Dr. Jennifer Hartstein, a child and adolescent psychologist in New York City, sees a reason for it:

> Children don't have the same inhibitions that adults do about putting themselves out there for all the world to see. As we grow older, we look to the external cues to provide us with information about what is "acceptable" which thwarts the whole creative and imaginative process.

See, somewhere, we lost it. Somewhere along the timeline of "I'm a kid and having fun" to "I'm an adult and working for a living," we lost that ability to dream, to imagine, to have fun. We decided that in order to be an adult, we were required to think like an adult, act like an adult, and work like an adult.

That's fine. Except there's no rule that says being an adult means we can't think like a child when we want to. Too many people forget that part.

A few years ago, one of my employees asked me how he could be more creative. Just like that—he said it to me: "How can I be more creative?"

That's kind of like asking, "How can I lose 30 pounds?" The answer is obvious—diet and exercise, burn more calories than you take in. But of course, that's much easier said than done.

I talked to my employee and asked him some questions about his life outside of the office. Where does he live (a studio on the Lower East Side of Manhattan); how does he get to work each day? (He walks two blocks, takes the train six stops, and walks three blocks to the office, stopping for a cup of coffee on the way.) What does he do for lunch (usually goes out and gets a slice or two of pizza unless he has meetings), etc. . . .

I told him that tomorrow, he's not allowed to do anything the normal way. I told him he had to get up an hour earlier, and walk to work. Tea, no coffee. He was then required to eat lunch somewhere else, preferably a diner where he could interact with the wait-staff. Then, instead of coming right back to the office, he was required to wander about Central Park for an hour.

I tried to throw him out of his rut.

He came back to the office around 3 P.M., and didn't look that different. He hadn't dropped 20 pounds, his hair wasn't parted in a different direction. But he had a subtle smile on his face. I asked him about it, and he told me why.

"I see the difference," he said. "I broke out of the day-to-day."

He had just learned to allow himself to be creative.

One of the things I like most about being in PR is that there's always something to outdo. There's always some new promotion, some new contest or event, some kind of stunt that we can try and do one better.

I would say that with the possible exception of the advertising world, we're in the industry that allows us to be the most creative.

Remember a few years ago, when Taco Bell floated a giant target in the middle of the ocean and said that if the Russian Space Station MIR hit it upon crashing down to earth, everyone in the United States would get a free taco? That was brilliant! They got tons and tons of press coverage from that stunt, and it raised the creativity bar a little higher for the rest of us.

That's the beauty of PR. You can always try to raise that bar a little higher. The question is threefold: How do you allow yourself to try and raise that bar, how do you sell it to the bosses, and then finally, how do you execute it?

Everyone has different ways of enhancing their creativity. In the end, like so many things, you'll need to find the best method that works for you specifically. Unlike, say, math, where 2 plus 2 will always equal 4, creativity doesn't really have steadfast rules. Each person makes up his own rules on how to be creative—what works for him might not work for another person.

The following rules are what work for me. I'm not saying you have to follow these rules, but they give you an idea of what you can look for. Tailor them to fit your lifestyle, and write your own rules.

PETER'S TOP SIX RULES FOR ALLOWING YOURSELF TO BE CREATIVE AND COME UP WITH OFF-THE-WALL IDEAS

1. *Get up, stand up. (Then jump around.)* Sitting in front of your computer and staring at the screen until blood droplets form on your forehead is not the way to get new ideas. Put Instant Messenger on "away mode," shut off the monitor, and walk away from the computer. Then put on a t-shirt, a pair of shorts, and some running shoes. Go for a walk. Or a run. Or a hop, skip, and a jump.

   For me personally, it's all about upping the endorphins. Endorphins are our friends.

   Bad day? Go for a run. Need a change but don't know what it needs to be? Stairmaster. Can't figure out how to get a client to understand that you're right and they're so most obviously wrong? Bench press. The key is to get your heart pumping, get moving, motivated, and head back into the office with a fresh brain. It does wonders, and it's been proven by scientists that the resulting high you get from a workout lasts well beyond the end of that workout.

2. *Overcome a fear, and stagnation goes out the window.* What scares you? I mean really scares you? I'm not talking about the old, "I'll touch this 9-volt battery to my tongue" fear, I'm talking REAL terror. What wouldn't you do in a million years? Perhaps it's skydiving. Perhaps it's bungee jumping, or even going to a nightclub wearing something that will land you in purgatory for eight years.

    Simply do it. Whatever it is, do it. I keep a "fear-tip-jar" in my office. Every day I dump excess change, a single or two, whatever I have around, into that jar. When it gets to the point where I feel like I'm dragging, or starting to stagnate, or simply losing it, I grab all that money, and go do something scary. So far, I've skydived, SCUBA dived, rock climbed, bungee jumped, and done a 180 in a modified police car while going 120 miles per hour. The incredible rush you get from that which makes your mother wince is sometimes exactly what you need to pull your creativity back from the brink of doom.

3. *Talk to a child, think like a child.* Did it ever occur to you that a six-year-old doesn't worry about the stock market? Or whether or not the Fed is going to raise interest rates, or whether another 20,000 layoffs are coming? Ever try to figure out why?

    Children live in the moment. Children don't understand the worry of anticipation, or the trauma of the "potential." Children know what's going on because they're seeing it happen in front of their eyes, and nowhere else. Talk to a child, think like a child.

    How to do it: find a child. A neighbor's kid, a brother's kid, they're all around you. Find one. Explain to the parents that you're more than willing to watch the kid for a few hours, giving the parents a well-deserved chance to relax and enjoy pampering themselves at the local mall.

    Turn off the cell phone. Turn off the pager. Turn off the computer. Get down on the floor with your little charge, and play. Do what he or she wants, whether it's having imaginary tea, or taking the Matchbox cars through the imaginary car wash. Ask questions! Ask why the purple car is going before the red car—the answers will amaze you! Remember them—they work in real life, too! As I said before, children don't think along the lines of a spreadsheet, or why x + y has to equal z. They simply do what's in their heads, right at that second. And that is a wonderful way to be.

4. *Walk a dog. Or a cat. Or a parrot. Or a llama.* Animals are wonderful beings in that they provide comfort, happiness, joy, and beauty to a sometimes superficial and cynical world. Animals, much like children, aren't ruled by schedules or day planners.

   Go take a dog to the park, or for a walk along the beach. Toss the stick, and watch the unabashed joy in their eyes as they haul butt to bring it back to you, tails going a thousand wags-per-minute. Try and remember that excitement level in them, where their whole body is just focused on the next throw of the stick: "Where's it gonna go? Am I gonna catch it? This is awesome!"

   No dog access? No worries, go to a zoo. Zoos are magical places that unfortunately, with the exception of fifth grade science class and the occasional fund-raiser, aren't used anywhere near enough by adults. Go inside. Walk through all the different lands. Watch the primates. Look at a monkey, and wonder how such a smart animal can look so stupid. Walk to the plains and check out the Hippo. He comes up for air, sinks back into the swamp. Comes up for air, sinks back into the swamp. Swats a fly, comes up for air . . . you get the idea.

   In fact, why not go to the local animal shelter and spend some time with one of the dogs or cats there? Just hang out with them. Talk to them. Walk with them. Give them some much-needed company, and in exchange, they'll take care of you, and help you think a little differently. (Plus, you might just wind up with a new housemate. Hey, it happened to me.)

5. *Finally, can't get out of your office at the moment, but still need a boost? Read things you've never read before.*

Sometimes we get so trapped in our little world, that even when we think we're being creative and different, we're still doing it inside our own comfort zone. We haven't escaped it, even when we think we have.

Living in New York City, there are certain magazines that I can tell you I rarely see on the shelves of the local news dealer. *Soldier of Fortune,* for instance. Or *Hunting Times.* Most New Yorkers don't really hunt in their spare time. ("I'll be back tonight, honey. I'm going to go bag a deer on 54th and Lexington.") so these magazines are kind of foreign to me. Sort of like NASCAR. While NASCAR might be huge in other parts of the country (Heck, it's huge even in other parts of the state!), it's not really my thing.

So to break out of that rut, I'll go spend twenty bucks and buy exactly that about which I'm clueless. Like *Soldier of Fortune* or a NASCAR magazine. For fun, I'll also buy a magazine that tells me how to decorate my motor home, or how to decorate the rims on my pimped-out ride. Mind you, I don't have a motor home, or a pimped-out ride. But that's exactly the point.

Reading these magazines serves many purposes for me. Not only do I learn something new, about which I was previously uninformed, but I also get out of my daily rut, my "read the *Wall Street Journal* and *BusinessWeek* only" rut. I focus on a new topic, creating new pathways in the brain where new information can go—information that might connect to other points of information and allow me to be a little more creative on all fronts.

Plus, I'm a much bigger hit at cocktail parties when I can switch from talking about the new budget for the 2006–2007 season to which motor homes have not only the best fuel economy, but also the widest sleeping berths, without missing a beat.

6. *A Bonus Rule: Work Somewhere Else*

With Wireless technology built into virtually every laptop nowadays, and with Wi-Fi hotspots in every coffee shop, airport, and stadium, there's no rule that says you're required to be at your desk.

I've held meetings from the most random of places–I've held brainstorming sessions in a forest; client pitches at amusement parks; and full-scale meetings, including charts and graphs, at an Italian restaurant on the Upper West Side. Get out of your office! Go work somewhere else for a day! Observe something other than the wall of your cubicle. It'll help change how you view the world. Sometimes during the summer, I bring my laptop up to the drop zone where I skydive. I work for an hour or so, then manifest myself onto a load and go fall out of a plane. I walk back, pack my parachute, and work for another hour. I do this four or five times over the course of a day.

Beats the hell out of a smoke-break.

My rules may not be exactly the same as your rules. That's the fun of it. They don't have to be! You can mix and match, you can make your own rules. Regardless, whatever you do to be more creative, be it playing with children or planting a garden, will let you come up with new and better ideas, allowing you to implement those ideas and generate terrific amounts of attention. (See Figure 3.1.)

Without question, it's fun to explore the child in you. It's what allows us to be creative, to come up with our great ideas, our spectacular promotions, and our tremendous events. By being creative and coming up with these off-the-wall ideas, you're putting all of your abilities to best use–you're using your creativity to make you, your company, or your clients stand out from the masses. And that's the goal.

But . . . in your quest to think differently–to be better, sharper, more creative than the masses–you're going to come up against a major problem, more often than you'd like. Here's a scenario that you'll have to face over and over again.

You've just come up with this spectacular idea. You went running in the park before work, and the idea just came to you

Figure 3.1 The author takes a few hours off at the Portland Zoo, in order to be a child. Portland, Oregon, 2005.

halfway between miles two and three. It's brilliant. It ties into your company or your client, and it's a definite press generator. It has merit, it's not just a stunt for the sake of being a stunt—it's about as close to perfect as you're gonna get.

So where's the problem?

Well, now you gotta sell it.

Remember: It's pretty much a given that there will be someone in your company or someone within your client's chain of command whose only job is to be a bean counter. He's the one they hired to keep costs down, expenses low . . . maybe even to protect the company from lawsuits.

He might be a lawyer, or a chief financial officer. Perhaps he's even a director with his eye on the bigger chair.

These people are what I call "Stoppers." Their job is to stop you. They know how to drain creativity faster than water flowing through the open holes in the *Titanic*. Their sole job is to keep things "status quo," and prevent anyone from ever going over that imaginary "boredom line."

Many great ideas have never made it past the Stopper. So many ideas have been shot dead by the Stopper, or not even brought to the Stopper's attention, because the person knew full well that the Stopper would win. Here's some shorthand on how to recognize the Stopper, as if you didn't already know the type!

Famous Stoppers

- Karl Rove
- Waylon Smithers (Mr. Burns' loyal sidekick on *The Simpsons*)
- Bill Lumbergh (Peter Gibbons' Boss in *Office Space*–The "Uh . . . Yeah . . ." guy)

Identifiable Traits of the Stopper

- Usually eats alone or with other Stoppers
- Usually has a bottle of Tums or Rolaids on his desk
- Never seen in a leopard-print tie
- Most likely not a skydiver or rock climber

I'm not totally putting the Stopper down. There's a purpose for his existence. Companies pay some Stoppers lots of money. Stoppers are spectacular in government and politics. They're the voice of humdrum existence everywhere–their job allows them the ability to say (in different terms, of course), "We can't become too exciting. We need to stay boring. Boring is safe."

You can, however, make a Stopper see your point of view, and sometimes, you can even make a Stopper a fan.

The key is being able to speak the Stopper's language.

I travel abroad a lot for work. When I'm on the plane, I always try and learn at least five basic phrases in the language spoken wherever it is I'm going. One of those phrases is always, "Please understand that I'm trying to learn your language, so I apologize in advance if I say anything incorrectly."

I know I won't be a master when I step off the tarmac, but perhaps I can learn just enough to let my gracious hosts know that I'm attempting to speak their language. That I'm making the effort to assimilate into their culture, instead of asking them to automatically assimilate into mine.

It's the same with the Stopper. You need to be able to speak the Stopper's language as you present your case for your super-creative idea.

I've learned that you should not speak softly. In fact, when attempting to get a Stopper to see things your way, you should ROAR. Here's how it works:

ROAR:

Responsibility

Opportunities

Awareness

Results

Stoppers are very finite people. They usually see things in black and white. You can identify them by their use of interrogative pronouns: Makes sense when you think about it—they're interrogating you to find out if what you're doing is good for the company. You job is to prove that it is. Expect to hear these types of questions from a Stopper:

- How much is this going to cost us?
- What are the legal ramifications?
- Can we get sued?
- How much money will this bring in?
- How many advertising dollars does this equate to?
- How many people will be involved?
- Where would it be done?
- Will there be insurance?

(That last one is my favorite.)

Real event, several years ago:

> "We're giving out dollar bills in Times Square to promote hand sanitizer. Why would we possibly need insurance?" I asked.
>
> "Well," said the Stopper, "What if you gave someone a dollar bill, and he got a paper cut and sued?"

He actually said that. I stared, open-mouthed.

To a Stopper, however, this was a totally normal, and even worse, *defensible* question!

Since you know who a Stopper is, and you know what kind of questions he's going to ask, you should already be prepared when you go in to meet with the Stopper to get your super-creative idea approved.

Again, the key is to speak the Stopper's language. The key is to ROAR. Here are they key elements of ROARing.

RESPONSIBILITY

Who is going to be managing this idea? How many people are you going to need? How much will they be paid? Will you have to hire outside staff? Where will you get the budget? Will the budget be a standard budget from this year, or are you going to have to take it from somewhere else? Are you planning for un-expected expenses? What about insurance? Workman's comp? If the event isn't being held here, where will you hold it? Do you need insurance there? What about permits?

The best way to deal with a Stopper's responsibility ques-tions is to make sure you have the answers to every possible question he could have, well before he has to ask it. By having all this information readily available for the Stopper, you'll shut him down—he won't have a leg to stand on, and your super-creative idea can move to phase two.

OPPORTUNITIES

Why are you creating this super-creative idea in the first place? Why do you want to implement it? What do you expect to get out of it? What positive opportunities are there for the company? How many? How will it improve the company's reputation? What kind of people will it attract? What kind of media attention will the company get out of it? Where will the media be? Will it be local or national or global? How much media coverage will it get in total? What is the advertising value of that media coverage? Will it be on the Web? Will there be photos? Will there be video? Will it be live or taped? Will it be covered live or sent out after the fact on video and background tape?

Again, preparedness is the key. But the difference here is that you're creating a lot of these answers out of thin air. No one can predict what kind of media coverage you're going to get. It might be the greatest story in the world, and every TV station within 300 miles may have agreed to send a crew and devote 11 minutes of their newscast to you. Then, an hour before your event starts, a bomb goes off downtown.

You can't control that. But you *can* take figures, numbers, and ideas from past promotions and events, and use them as a baseline or a guide. Remember, this is a really good time to under-promise and over-deliver. I used to have a client who swore by under-promising and over-delivering to his clients. He said it made him look like a hero. Scotty, the Chief Engineer from the original *Star Trek,* said the same thing to Geordi, the Chief Engineer of *Star Trek: The Next Generation.* After Geordi tells Captain Picard the REAL time that it would take to complete a task, Scotty remarks, "Oh, laddie. You got a lot to learn if you want the people to think of you as a miracle worker."

Your goal is to be a miracle worker for the Stopper. Do it once, he'll never stop you again. Under-promise and over-deliver. Write down exactly what you hope to get out of this super-creative idea, then scale it back by a fourth. Have all the answers to the Stopper's potential questions written down, and go into that meeting ready for action.

AWARENESS

Awareness can be a super-creative person's best defense against a good Stopper. Awareness allows you to show the Stopper that you're on top, not only of the situation at hand, but of any problems that can possibly come up. Awareness shows the Stopper that you've got a tremendous knowledge of *not only* your super-creative idea, but all the potential pitfalls and hazards that could derail not only your event, but the entire client or company.

A Stopper doesn't see "A great event that will bring totally great press to the client!" A Stopper sees "A hundred media outlets, all outside in the parking lot, all waiting for something to go wrong that they can beam, in full color, all around the world."

Awareness shows the Stopper that you see that, too. When coupled with Responsibility and Opportunities, Awareness lets the Stopper relax a little bit. It takes his guard down ever so slightly, and tells him, "It's ok to listen to this super-creative idea, because the person who thought it up took into account anything that could possibly go wrong and hurt us."

At this point, it's sort of like feeding a wild chipmunk a nut. He knows it's a nut, knows he wants it, but he's still a little hesitant in taking it from your hand. That leads us to our final strategy.

RESULTS

When you think of showing results to a client, a boss, or even a Stopper, you think of putting together a PowerPoint presentation or a book when the project ends, showing what you did, how you did it, what you did right and wrong, what were the successes and failures, and so on.

But for a Stopper, results are not a one-time event. Results need to happen daily. Results (to paraphrase Gordon Gekko in the movie *Wall Street*) clarify, cut through, and capture. Results allow a Stopper to process where the project is, how it's going, and what happens next. They calm the Stopper down. They're the Stopper's Valium.

Always be ready with results for the Stopper. Get the permit from the city to hold the event on 26th Street. Scan it and include it in an "update" email to the Stopper. Let him know where you are, what you're doing, and what the very next steps are. Show the Stopper that you are on top of the project every step of the way. You're not hiding anything from the Stopper, you're not afraid to show him exactly what you're up to, any time of day. If the Stopper walks in to your office at 9:42 on a Tuesday morning, or 11:35 on the Thursday night before the event, you're more than willing to show him exactly where you are, the status of the project, and what it's doing at this very finite moment in time.

This keeps the Stopper happy. It makes him feel better. It makes him calm.

Of course, when the actual event *is* over, you'll prepare your usual results book–media clips, stories, video, transcripts. Also, you'll turn in a final budget of how much you spent versus how much you predicted you'd spend. (You did come in under budget, right? Under-promising and over-delivering, remember?)

But, because you've been offering the Stopper results since the project started, you now have the ability to present a much bigger results book. You can show the Stopper exactly what you've done since the beginning.

This in turn, will make the Stopper a fan. You've proven you know what you're doing, and you've shown the Stopper that you're one of those rare breeds of Creative Genius who also has the ability to back up his ravings with facts, figures, and results.

You've turned the Stopper into a friend. Your next idea will fly through approvals in about 11 seconds.

Oh, and don't be surprised when the Stopper asks you to join him for lunch.

WHAT WE LEARNED
FROM THIS CHAPTER

1. The Off-the-Wall idea can be the best one. It can vault you from obscurity to national attention in the blink of an eye. But first, you have to be able to come up with it. You have to be creative.

2. To be creative, you have to do different things than you're doing right now. You have to change various parts of you, and act in ways not normally associated with your regular routine. By doing this, you're ensuring positive change within yourself.

3. You can take that positive change and utilize it in coming up with a great new super-creative idea. But to then implement that idea, you need to get it past the Stoppers.

4. To talk to the Stoppers, you have to ROAR: Responsibility, Opportunity, Awareness, Results. By having answers to any and all possible questions a Stopper will throw at you, you're setting yourself up for success.

5. Under-promise and over-deliver to the Stopper. By doing this, and creating a results book along the way, you'll prove to the Stopper that you can be trusted with the big idea. You can be counted on to deliver, that you have creativity, but also have the ability to implement that creativity responsibly. In short, you'll prove you're "good for the company."

?!

CHAPTER 4

Coming Up with and Implementing the Big Idea—Part One

WEBDIVE 2000: THE INTERNET COMMUNITY'S FIRST-EVER SKYDIVING TRIP

So let me set the scene for you. It's just about the summer of 2000. Right in the heyday of the dotcom boom. Everyone, and I mean everyone, is trying to get involved in the Internet industry in some form. People are either coming up with ridiculous business plans and getting them funded (think online pet cemeteries, or virtual trash exchanges), or working in industries that support the dotcom boom.

Back in those days, no matter what was happening, people wanted in, and they wanted people to know about them. And to do that, some people were coming up with crazier and crazier publicity stunts to promote themselves.

What was happening was a constant, ever-growing race to be louder. To make more noise, to get more exposure, to get more ink, to please the investors. The goal was constant noise.

The problem is, with constant noise comes very little signal. It's kind of tough to differentiate yourself from the masses by jumping up and down, when everyone else is jumping up and down, too.

Like dotcom companies, PR firms were enjoying the wild ride. Most agencies were growing like wildfire during the boom, with some agencies doubling, tripling, even quadrupling in size. The Geek Factory, between 1999 and 2001, added 11 people to our payroll. We were growing just like the other agencies. And just like the other agencies, there was no shortage of clients waiting to be taken on.

They came from everywhere. All over the country, and all around the world. The mantra of the dotcom era (other than IPO! IPO!) was "Get known."

Every company's business plan had a section devoted to "PR." And it wasn't just a passing mention, either. The dotcom era was when companies truly learned the value of a well-crafted public relations plan.

Whereas PR had once occupied the low-respect zone of "something that we use if we have a crisis," it quickly turned into something required in every facet of the company. It happened virtually overnight.

You know that saying about the shoemaker's kids not having any shoes? Or the piano tuner's home piano being completely off-key? Well, it was happening in the PR industry, too.

PR firms were spending so much time on all this new business, both handling new clients coming in and dealing with the ones they currently had, that very few firms were remembering to market *themselves!*

While in some cases there wasn't a huge need to (i.e., for the most part during the dotcom era, PR firms had more business than they could handle, anyway), in the end, agencies still needed to get their names out there.

While most of The Geek Factory's clients came from existing client recommendations (which is still the case, and still flatters us), we found that our nontraditional way of thinking was beginning to be copied by other agencies. Companies were realizing that old-school, thousand-employee PR firms just weren't quick enough for the dotcom pace, and were turning to smaller "out-of-the-box" firms.

Since The Geek Factory was one of the leaders in the out-of-the-box attitude, we started thinking that it might be a good idea to do a stunt for *ourselves* for a change. While we were doing tons for our clients–for instance, setting up a boxing ring at a black-tie function and having Muhammad Ali, Roberto Duran, and other famous boxers hang out and trade punches with industry leaders–we kept thinking that it would be a good idea to do something on our own.

We wanted to do something that not only showcased our ability to get media attention for our clients, but something that showed the way we thought. We wanted to come up with an idea that would bring together all the aspects of what our agency was and the best traits of our employees.

But what could we do? How do you come up with a super-creative idea when it's not about a client, but about you? When you're spending all your time focusing on getting your clients into the news, it's kind of a shock to the system to take a step back and say, "Ok, for the next hour, it needs to be about us."

What we learned is that we're no different than any other client. We just weren't treating ourselves that way.

In the end, our job is to create "tellable" stories out of whatever we're given to work with. Most of the time, that's easy. You have a story; you can work with the client to craft it, and work with the reporter to pitch it.

Most of the time. Most of the time, publicists have a specific target where they want to pitch their story. Financial client? The financial publications. Consumer client? The consumer publications. Sure, you have to put your creative thinking caps on like we discussed, but the basics, the very foundation of what we know–get a client, get media–is there.

When it's you, it's not that simple. For instance . . . we're trying to tell the world who we are. Well, we're a PR agency. Ok. So we should pitch to magazines that cover the PR world. Well, there's . . . um . . . one. Maybe two.

And are the right people reading those magazines? Doubtful. Are the marketing directors reading the PR magazines? Possibly–but most likely not. PR magazines are read almost exclusively by publicists and PR agencies.

Ok, so they're out. What else?

This is what we did as an agency as we tried to figure out how to pitch ourselves. We went through every possible scenario, and tried to figure out how we could position ourselves in there. We learned some valuable lessons, most of which we knew, but were thankful to get them reinforced into our brains:

> **Rule #1:** PR for the sake of PR is a waste of time. Consequently, a PR stunt for the sake of a PR stunt is a waste of time.

> **Rule #2:** If you're going to pitch a story to a media outlet that normally wouldn't cover you, make sure the story is so hot, they'll *want* to cover you. Since you're already fighting the fact that they don't normally pay you any attention, your story has to be just that much better.

> **Rule #3:** Treat yourself as a client. Don't come up with ideas that you'd be ashamed to present to a paying client. You are a paying client—your time is valuable. It's time that could be spent billing. If you're not coming up with ideas that are up to the same scale to which you hold your ideas for clients, you're wasting your time.

> **Rule #3a:** Since the goal of promoting yourself is to increase your positive brand and by extension, increase your business, anything you do during the time you're working on yourself that is substandard or not to par doesn't only waste your time, but it costs you money.

Once we realized that we needed to treat ourselves as a client, the whole process seemed to make a lot more sense.

We're a client, and as such, deserve the same creative input that we'd give any other client.

After we figured that out, the ideas started flowing:

> Ok—we're a PR firm, but a nontraditional one. We're not afraid to take risks. We're willing to go the extra mile, not because it's expected, but because we enjoy it. We get off on this—we love coming up with and implementing ideas for our clients. When the clients buy in and the ideas come to fruition, that's when we're happiest. It's like a drug . . . we're good press junkies. We need our constant fix. We're . . . media adrenaline junkies.

With every sentence that came out of that brainstorm, so rose a clearer vision of what we needed to do to promote ourselves. It wasn't about us promoting The Geek Factory as a PR firm where clients would have great success, it was promoting *ourselves as the agency that loves what they do!* That was the differential!

Every agency out there says they'll get you good press. They say they're good at it. They say they're constantly there for their clients, and are always willing to go the extra mile.

But few, if any, ever come out and tell the clients that they're actually *addicted* to the feeling they get when they create a successful campaign! Too many agencies say, "Oh, we're exceptionally good at creating campaigns for X, Y, and Z."

That's great—but wouldn't you rather work with an agency that NEEDS to do that? An agency for whom coming up with those ideas is not required because the clients want it, but because without it, the agency can't feed its addiction?

If the agency is addicted to the feeling they get from delivering those kinds of creative successes to the client, I'd say the client is going to be very happy with the quality and quantity of work that agency is putting out. Wouldn't you agree?

Well, that was the bolt of lightning we needed. All of a sudden, our agency had a mantra. We were addicted to the results we got for our clients. And then the ideas started flowing.

?!?!?!?!?!?!?!?

> **Rule:** Figure out what your company's or agency's addiction is. What makes you tick, what makes you grow, what makes you happy? Focus on that—it's what you're going to do best anyway. Tell *that* story. That's the story you'll be most passionate about, that's the story that your passion will tell *for* you. If a reporter "gets" that passion, sees it in you, the story becomes that much more compelling.

So then, after deciding that we were going to push the addiction angle, it was a question of how best to tell that story inside of an event. What could you do to truly show addiction to positive press?

We started brainstorming on all the *positive* ways we liked to fulfill that "high," as it were. In our office there were runners. Some had completed marathons, one had even done an ultra-marathon. Amazing accomplishments, no doubt–but you couldn't very well invite 150 reporters to go run a half-marathon, could you?

One employee was a mountain climber. Great. Again, though, we didn't really see the small business editor at the *Financial Times* summiting Kilimanjaro with us anytime soon.

We took a break from the brainstorm, and one employee and I went downstairs to get a soda. I remember exactly what she said. She said, "What we need is something thrilling that doesn't require anyone to be in triathlete shape, but will be remembered long after it's over."

We both stopped in mid-gulp. We swallowed, and looked at each other.

"Skydiving," we both said simultaneously.

WebDive 2000 was born right in the middle of one Diet Pepsi and one Diet Dr. Pepper.

?!?!?!?!?!?!?!?

> **Rule:** Never forget, not even for a moment, that what you do for a living doesn't respect the 9-to-5. You don't work in an industry where at 5:01 P.M.,
>
> *(continued)*

?!?!?!?!?!?!?!?

you can shut-off your monitor and go home. You work in an industry of creativity, and neither you, your employees, your bosses, nor anyone else has any control over where that creativity will strike. Always, always, always be ready to capitalize on it.

Running back upstairs, we both burst into the office. "Skydiving!" we shouted. "Let's take everyone skydiving!"

As anyone who has ever worked for me in the past knows, there's a moment in time between which I suggest one of my insane/creative ideas and everyone else in the room "gets it." At The Geek Factory, this is called "Peter-time." It's those few seconds where you finish talking, you're excited, you're passionate, you've just given the idea of a lifetime to a room full of people, and they're looking at you like you just told them you were a spotted owl.

It usually takes anywhere from three to five seconds for people to process what you just said. When the idea is really, really out there, it might take a few seconds longer.

So it kind of went like this, that day at The Geek Factory.

"We're gonna take everyone skydiving!"

Pause. Pause. Pause. Pause. Pause. Pause. Pause.

"Oh, cool!"

?!?!?!?!?!?!?!?

Rule: Hold your ground. Finish the idea, and wait for the response. Don't shrink back or shirk away just because you don't get applause within .002 seconds of the last syllable. If the idea is wild enough, and you've come up with all the answers to your Stoppers, you'll get the applause. It just takes mortals a few seconds longer to process super-creative ideas than it takes us.

Of course, in our situation, when it finally sank into our staff's heads that they were going to have to jump out of an airplane as well, it set off some interesting conversations. But that's neither here nor there.

Once we decided what we were going to do, everything shifted into ultra-high gear. It was late May. We planned the event for July 22, 2000.

Our first major hurdle (or so we thought) would be convincing a hundred leaders in the New York New Media community to jump out of a plane with us.

With no warning whatsoever, we posted the same message to a bunch of mailing lists one day in late May:

> Want to jump out of a plane? The Geek Factory is thinking of organizing a giant Skydiving Day for Silicon Alley area people. Interested? Email us.

We crossed our fingers and hit send.

Three hours later, we'd filled up 100 spots, and had a waiting list almost as long.

At that point, we realized that not only did we have something here, but we could produce an amazing event, complete with more press coverage than we ever dreamed. An event that would not only solidify The Geek Factory as one of the major "event" PR agencies out there, but definitely as one of the most creative.

And hey, if it meant I had to jump out of a plane for the first time in my life, so be it. We all make sacrifices for our profession.

As the event started to take shape, it quickly started becoming known as the "event to be at." We were getting calls from tons of Silicon Alley denizens, asking if they could join us. Unfortunately, based on the number of planes they had at the drop zone, we had a finite cap on the amount of participants.

We started calling some of the bigger companies that had joined us, and asked for "donations" to make our event even better. A senior artist at Deutsch Advertising came up with a spectacular logo for us, and WebDive 2000 had an image! (See Figure 4.1.)

We told all our jumpers that if they wanted to participate and get some additional recognition, they needed to come up with nontraditional things to put in the gift bags–things that would help our event stand out even more. We wanted people to have tangible things to take home, other than the rush of adrenaline that we knew they'd get. We wanted WebDive 2000 to be (as we're famous for saying) remembered, not simply recalled.

The Geek Factory Inc. Presents...

Mike Dreeland 2000

Figure 4.1 Webdive 2000.

> **Rule:** Give people the task of being creative for a good cause and, 99 percent of the time, they will.

One company donated over 100 disposable cameras. Another came in with foot cream (for soft landings, of course). T-shirts, beer, food, you name it–companies stepped up to be a part of this awesome event.

> **Rule:** Get one company on board. Use them as a springboard: "Well, company X has joined us. Surely they wouldn't have joined us if this wasn't going to be a spectacular event."

We predicted that if we didn't tell the media, but rather, let it filter down, it would be a much stronger story. After all, what reporter doesn't want to "discover" something without anyone else's help?

Sure enough, within four days of our initial announcement, the reporters started calling: *BusinessWeek, Forbes, PR Week, The Silicon Alley Reporter, @NY,* the NY *Daily News.* All calling, asking pretty much the same question:

> Um, yeah, we're trying to confirm a rumor we've been hearing: Is The Geek Factory really planning on throwing 100 industry leaders out of a plane?

One reporter got in touch with the law firm that represented us. Our attorney, of course, had no comment, but certainly had one for us, when the phone rang a minute later.

"Peter, are you out of your $%@! MIND?"

Not having a board to which we had to answer, we didn't have any Stoppers in our way, but our training had served us well. We placated our attorney with numbers: The number of people killed in tandem skydiving accidents was so small, there were barely any records. Insurance companies knew this, and it wouldn't affect us as a company at all.

While I can't say he was thrilled, he was certainly relieved to find that out. He still insisted on drafting a waiver for every participant to sign, and we agreed.

?!?!?!?!?!?!?!?!?!?

> **Rule:** Lawyers and Stoppers, while circumventable on many occasions, really are there to protect you. If they occasionally don't let you get away with something, regardless of how well you've done your ROAR, then there's probably a good reason for it. That said, you should still always attempt a compromise.

WebDive 2000 could go on as scheduled, with the simple addition of a liability waiver . . . a win on all counts.

As we continued to count down the days until the big drop, we got another surprise: A few of the stories that had already run had talked about The Geek Factory as this "event planning and PR firm in New York City." Well, people started reading, and we started getting phone calls:

> Hi, we're from company XYZ, and we're looking for a truly unique event that will separate us from the masses at the next industry trade show in about six months. Do you want to come in and present some ideas?

We had come up with WebDive 2000 as a way to promote The Geek Factory. Why should we have been surprised to find that it was actually working?

The first body hadn't even fallen from the plane yet, and WebDive 2000 was paying massive dividends. Not surprisingly, of all the companies that called, none of them wanted us to throw them or their customers out of planes.

?!?!?!?!?!?!?!?

Rule: Say yes, and figure out when you'll find the time to do it later.

As we counted down to the final day, as people started calling with questions, and as we kept figuring out more and more ways to squeeze in the continued stream of journalists who kept asking to get added to the list, we realized we had another problem in the office.

We were all scared beyond belief of jumping out of a plane.

Looking back on it, it's pretty amazing that the entire staff agreed to do it. All of my employees knew they could say no at any time. It most definitely was not a mandatory company function. I'd certainly never jumped before, and I was as scared as anyone else. Couldn't admit that, obviously, but in the rush and resulting craziness of putting this entire event together, I never stopped to think—"Hey, you're going to be exiting a plane at approximately 13,500 feet and plummeting at around 120 miles an hour to the ground. Are you sure you're up to this?"

Fortunately, stress is a great equalizer. It lets you forget rather quickly what's coming next, and instead focus on the present. We knew we'd have to jump, but we also had to produce this event, which was quickly consuming our lives and becoming a massive stunt, bigger than anything we'd produced to date. That was kind of scary. Fortunately, we knew how to handle it.

?!?!?!?!?!?!?!?

> **Rule:** Much like skydiving, if you fracture your professional life into micro-bursts—quick time periods—instead of being awed and frightened by the magnitude of it all, you're forced to focus on just that which is in the present—right now—and handle it. This is exceptionally good for crisis management, and long road races of over 13.1 miles.

The day arrived. On very little sleep, we met our 100 or so jumpers at 5 A.M. in Midtown Manhattan. Boarding school busses, they all signed their waivers, got their goody bags, and settled in for the two-hour drive to the drop zone.

There was nervous chatter on the bus. I remember forcing myself to listen to what other people were saying, and getting instant feedback. One thing I found very interesting was when people asked each other how they found out about it. The general consensus was, "I dunno. A friend told me."

Apparently, the groundswell of buzz around WebDive 2000 was huge—everyone had found out from a friend, or a friend of a friend. Emails were forwarded throughout offices, instant messages were traded back and forth. For as much as we knew, no one even saw the initial email request to the Internet mailing lists, but rather, heard it from friends who got the email from friends who got the email from friends. . . .

?!?!?!?!?!?!?!?

> **Rule:** Keep it simple, clean, and to the point. Let the email take on a life of its own; let the announcement do the work for you. Why take out an ad if you don't need to? Why ruin your voice shouting it from the rooftops? If your message is compelling enough, people will shout it from the rooftops *for* you.

Another Rule: Listen to the winds. People talk. They talk everywhere. If not on a bus, then on message boards. Via email. In locker rooms. In cafeterias. ABL: Always Be Listening. You never know what you'll hear, and you never know who will be saying it.

As the busses pulled into the drop zone, the noise died down, and the magnitude of what we were all about to do really hit home. It's one thing to talk with your friends and joke, "Oh, yeah, tomorrow I'm jumping out of a perfectly good airplane"; it's quite another to look over, see a grass field and two Cessna 182s sitting there, idling quietly.

More than one person came over to me and said, "How did I get talked into this? You must be a really good PR firm to make us want to do this." More than one person also looked a bit pale. But there was no turning back now.

All hundred of us got our mass briefing from the owner of the drop zone, who told us that while the tandem masters who were strapped to our backs would be doing most of the work, we still had to follow some basic procedures, such as arching our backs, not touching anything we weren't supposed to touch, and the like.

Quite the wake-up call.

However, as the first person touched the ground safely under 400 feet of canopy, the nervousness evaporated, and the fearful chatter turned to shouts of "I'm next!"

Finally, after an injury-free 104 jumps, it was the last jump of the day–my jump. The pilot said he'd give me a little extra altitude, to thank me for bringing all this business to his drop zone. "Um, that's ok, really," I think I replied.

As I watched another jumper (a fun jumper, they call them) get sucked over the side of the Cessna before me, I smiled, and got surprisingly calm. Much like setting a good plan into motion, I was strapped to my tandem master, and he was exiting the plane with me, whether I wanted to go or not. I didn't have much of a choice anymore, and all I could do was hold on and enjoy the ride.

I felt the wind in my face, heard "READY!" in my ear, and closed my eyes. Next thing I remember was thinking "This will really be an amazing PR stunt, if I get to the ground in one piece."

After that, the canopy opened, as did my eyes, and it was all very much real.

To this day, I watch the video they gave me of my jump, and my parents swear that the look of fear in my eyes was the same one I had the first time I went on stage to perform when I was seven years old. I vehemently disagree, but hey, they probably know better than me.

> **Rule:** After the event ends, before you write the post-op report, before you brief the client the next day, GET SOME SLEEP. Your body, your brain, and all your sensibilities will thank you.

Fourteen hours later, I woke up to a ringing phone. It was *BusinessWeek*. They were planning on doing a story on the event; did I have time for a brief interview?

I smiled. We had a winner.

It was definitely one of the most fun post-operation reports I've ever written. (And yes, we did one on the event, even though it was our own event. It made it crystal clear what our clients expect from them.)

Things we did right included:

1. **Letting the email drive itself, allowing people to forward on the original email to fill up the list.** (Keep in mind, people paid for this themselves. We didn't lay out a penny.)
2. **Realizing that the resulting buzz from the initial email was what really drove the actual event.** People stayed at the drop zone for close to 12 hours, talking, making friends, hanging out. The actual jumps took maybe 20 or 30 minutes, tops.

People brought their own cameras, which turned into people documenting the event on their own. This was in 2000, when very few people blogged. These days, an event like this would be online within minutes of the first person touching the ground.

Rule: Use citizen journalism to your advantage. Always let people photograph, blog, cover, write about, or video your events. When they do, they like to show it. They're becoming citizen publicists for you, free of charge. Make sure you work out the legalities of the filming, though. If you have celebrities or the event is in a private venue, make sure it's cleared first.

Of course, the media stories were spectacular. *BusinessWeek* did a full-page story online, the reporter telling about her experiences in the first person.

PR Week magazine, while bailing out of the actual jump, citing "bad back," and "acute cowardness," gave us the headline "When These Geeks Say Jump, Bring Your Business Card," and the first line of the article said, "Want to find out what your clients and media contacts are really made of? Jump out of a plane with them."

In the end, it was a truly successful event for so many different reasons. We got spectacular coverage and a host of new clients. We got a great story we can tell forever, as did every single jumper out that day.

Reporters learned that we were truly creative, and a trifle insane, and we've made friendships that have lasted to this day with some of the reporters who floated gently down to earth that day.

Perhaps the best thing to come from that experience? My first skydive was made that day, July 22, 2000. I figured I'd jump, get it over with, and move on.

I never expected to get hooked.

I'm currently a licensed skydiver, with over 120 solo jumps to my credit. It's the one time for me when I'm not answering email, talking on the phone, or dealing with clients. We should all have moments like that.

It's my one time just for me. Who ever thought it would come from a publicity stunt?

WHAT WE LEARNED
FROM THIS CHAPTER

1. Ideas come to you when you least expect them: be ready. Not only ready to write down the idea, but ready to act on it immediately.

2. Once you put an idea into motion, you can't just "stop and get off." Be prepared for that, too.

3. Offer incentives to people within the event to make it even better. In this case, we let attendees decide what should be in the gift bag as a way of promoting their specific companies through our event. It worked, they got press mentions out of it.

4. Treat yourself as a client—when promoting yourself or your own company, do it the same way you would if you were a client. Make sure you give yourself the same time and resources you would allot to a client. After all, you're "paying" for your time in other ways—don't waste it.

5. Sometimes you need to offer up potential compromises to your Stoppers that make everyone happy. In this case, it was including a liability waiver. A small price to pay to allow the event to happen.

6. Remember the feeling you had when you had your "Eureka!" moment about the idea in the first place. Don't lose it. The passion you have for an idea that you want to turn into an event needs to be there the entire way through, otherwise you might find yourself losing the drive and determination that got you there in the first place.

7. Finally, don't forget to point your chest toward the relative wind, take a deep breath, exit the plane, and arch.

?!

CHAPTER 5

Coming Up with and Implementing the Big Idea—Part Two

THE FLYING FINGERS YARN BUS—ARE THOSE KNITTING NEEDLES IN THE CENTER LANE?

Let's start this chapter off with a rule:

?!?!?!?!?!?!?!?

> **Rule: Always take the meeting. You never know where the next client, next big project, next crazy idea, next new job, next promotion, raise, or shot at glory is going to come from. Always, always take the meeting.**

In mid-2004, the agency gets an email to the bat-account (like the bat-phone, it's the hotline for potential new clients, only it's email).

"Hi there. We have a small knitting store about 20 miles outside of Manhattan. We'd like to talk to someone there about helping us promote it. Please call. Thanks."

As we found out later, they'd called six other agencies. We were the first (and only) ones to call them back. And we called them back within 20 minutes. That impressed the heck out of them, right there.

?!?!?!?!?!?!?!?!?

> Rule: Designate a specific email account or phone number as the bat-line—always have someone monitoring it—and respond ASAP. You'll land 90 percent of your business by being the first responder. It works every time. Companies, especially small companies, are amazed when PR agencies call them back right away. They never expect it.

Their email was pretty much on target—a husband-and-wife team owned a small knitting store outside Manhattan, in the town of Irvington, NY, called Flying Fingers Yarn Shop (FFYS). They were well known in the (no pun intended) tight-knit knitting community, but other than that, nada. Also, their big problem was getting people to visit their store. Irvington isn't the biggest community on the Hudson River, and even though the store was a block from the Metro-North light rail system, people didn't find it convenient or worthwhile to come up from the city.

In addition, I should explain to readers from outside of New York that New York City can be divided into two sections: below 96th Street, and "upstate." People who live in Manhattan tend to consider anything above 96th Street as "upstate," and rarely venture that way. Very few people in Manhattan have cars, because it's a city of walkers. As such, it wasn't surprising that FFYS was having a major problem attracting buyers.

My first thought, as I took the light rail up to meet with Kevin and Elise, was that they were going to be a really, really small client. But that was OK, sometimes really small clients can make for great campaigns, as well. Small clients mean less management teams, less approvals needed, less restrictions on what we can and can't do. Sometimes, small clients are the best clients to have!

As I got off the train in Irvington, and walked up the hill to their store, I tried to keep an open mind. "It's a small store," I thought. "But that's OK. We can do really fun small things for them."

Walking in, I immediately noticed some of the coolest yarn I've ever seen—yarn made from hemp, alpaca, soy (Yes! Tofu yarn!), and even bamboo. Really great stuff, all designed to make knitting exciting and fun, and a heck of a lot cooler than Grandma sitting in her rocking chair and passing the time.

I liked Kevin and Elise immediately. Right away, they "got" what PR can and can't do. They weren't expecting miracles, but rather, knew that PR is a process that takes time, and when done right, can yield spectacular results.

Based on the size of the store, I did, however, make one initial mistake. In my mind, I'd already written them off as a small client—not a bad thing, but a small client with a small retainer, and an even smaller budget for stunts or events.

I quickly learned otherwise.

> **Rule: Never assume that just because a company seems small, they don't have any money.**

I found out that Elise ran the store full-time, as did Kevin. When we started talking about ideas, I noticed that they were grandiose ideas—they were totally open to my way of thinking— "Oh, we should do this," or "Oh, we should do that," and Kevin and Elise were all like, "Yeah! That sounds great! Let's do it!"

Finally, I had to steer the meeting back into reality: "Um, just so you know, these are spectacular ideas, but perhaps we should consider starting off a little smaller, just from a funding angle," I suggested.

Well, as it turns out, Kevin had just retired from his position of extreme power at an investment firm. Not only could they afford The Geek Factory, but they could afford any stunts we could dream up, 75 times over.

"Ah." I said. "Well . . . let me go back to the office and put together a proposal."

On the train back into the city, I was positively giddy from excitement—the stuff we could do for them! Not only because they had a budget. Heck, that was the least of the reasons. For me, it was because they were so gung-ho over PR, and believed in the concept of stunts and events, and what good press could get you.

?!?!?!?!?!?!?!?

> **Rule: Regardless of budget, the kind of company you want to work with is one that wants to work *with you*. It's a very simple concept: if a company or a client understands the value proposition in PR and in stunts and events, and is willing to let you have creative freedom in order to get results, MAKE THEM A CLIENT!**

I started sketching out ideas on what we could do. My first challenge was to differentiate Flying Fingers. There were yarn shops all over the world—why were they different? Why should New Yorkers leave the cocoon of Manhattan and drag themselves out to Irvington, of all places? What purpose could it serve?

?!?!?!?!?!?!?!?

> **Rule: When you're dealing with a company that has many imitators, find out what makes them entirely different. Capitalize on that; promote that first, the company second.**

I made up a list.

Differences

- *Small store:* husband-and-wife owned—not an "impersonal big-city store."
- *Free advice:* come in; learn to knit.
- *Day excursion:* turn "having to leave the city" into "Ooh! We get to leave the city!"
- *Exclusivity:* Yarns there available nowhere else.

Taking all that into account, we figured that the best way to start a PR campaign for Flying Fingers was to do a little bit of everything, and then some. We came up with two campaigns, the first of which was the "Eat Your Sweater" email.

Basically, we sent an email to long-lead editors, advising them that while they all knew how hot knitting was (we coined the phrase "Knitting is the new Pilates") they might not have known that the new hotness *in* knitting was all about knitting with nontraditional yarns.

The pitch was simple and to the point. It was June of 2004, and the holiday press was starting to ramp up. Christmas press is amazing–they start earlier and earlier every year. Eventually, they're going to start next year's research on December 26. Mark my words.

Anyhow, the pitch went something like this:

?!

Dear <editor name>:

Pop-culture holiday season gift: Knitting with nontraditional yarn is the new Pilates.

Save our Sheep. Knit with cooler stuff. I'm talking about really funky yarn—ALPACA—TOFU (Soy Yarn! Seriously! You can eat your sweater!!)

Brace yourself—BAMBOO! I'm wearing a sweater made out of bamboo yarn right now. It's unbelievably soft. Wild, wild stuff.

Flying Fingers Yarn Shop (www.flyingfingers.com). Also in physical space in Irvington, NY, the largest "weird" yarn store in the entire world.

Tons of off-the-wall yarn, over 4,000 types.

Coolest part? They have, on their site, a $9.95 special—soy yarn, needles, tape measure, and instructions on how to make a scarf. You can turn anyone into a knitter this holiday season!

Shoot me an email. Call me. I'll send you free yarn—bamboo? Tofu?

You name it. Knit to your heart's content.

Thanks for reading!

—Peter Shankman
(for Flying Fingers)

?!

Simple, to the point, and direct, this pitch went out to about 400 holiday editors and reporters around the country. We got about a 40 percent response rate–pretty good for holiday. The story ran in lots of craft gift publications, but also on several morning shows (the concept of people eating their sweater was too good of a visual to pass up, I suppose) as well as long-lead magazines that had Christmas gift lists.

?!?!?!?!?!?!?!?

> **Rule:** It's never too early to start thinking about how you're going to pitch your client for holiday publications. And even if your client is a nonconsumer item, ask yourself if there's anything they can do to get into the gift lists and magazines for the upcoming holiday season.

In the end, we got a really decent amount of press that we knew would be coming out around Christmas time, 2004. We were happy, and Flying Fingers was happy.

But that was still four months away! What could we do for right NOW?

?!?!?!?!?!?!?!?

> **Rule:** Don't ever stop. We work in an industry that doesn't "end" just because we got some media attention. There's always more to get. Figure out different ways of getting it.

It was right about the time of the 2004 Republican Convention, and New York City was bracing for the traffic nightmare to end all traffic nightmares. The city powers-that-be had placed a "frozen zone" into effect, covering major streets and avenues around Madison Square Garden. This was going to cause a lot of trouble, congestion, and people sitting in their cars, with nothing to do for hours on end.

That's when our first burst of creativity hit: Use the traffic to our advantage!

We called Flying Fingers, and asked them to create a few thousand "Learn to Knit in Traffic Kits." In these kits, we wanted a pair of knitting needles, a ball of yarn, a pattern of a donkey and an elephant, and a one-page primer on how to knit.

We called contacts we knew at New York University, and told them we needed eight students to help hand these kits out all around the frozen zone during the convention. Not only do students love jobs like this, but getting paid for doing something fun doesn't hurt, either.

We even made t-shirts for the NYU students to wear. On the front, they said Flying Fingers. On the back, the words "Donkeys, Elephants, and New Yorkers! Oh, My!" We dressed our NYU students up in the shirts, and sent them out around the perimeter of the frozen zone, handing out thousands of these kits to unsuspecting drivers. They told the drivers, "Hey, you're stuck in traffic with nothing else to do, why not learn to knit?"

The first day, we sent the kids out all over the perimeter. They handed out about a thousand kits. The kits, mind you, cost virtually nothing to make; they were surprisingly cheap. So from a return-on-investment standpoint, we didn't have that far to go.

> **Rule: When you're testing out a campaign or stunt for the first time, try and do it with items that don't cost that much to begin with. If it fails miserably, you haven't lost a lot. If it succeeds wildly, you've made a small fortune.**

At around 7:30 A.M. the second day, before the NYU students arrived at the office to pick up the second batch of kits, I got a call from Elise, letting me know that she received a voice mail from someone in a car who had gotten a kit from "a very excited 20-year-old," and thought they were wonderful. Would Flying Fingers want to create a few hundred branded kits for her daughter's upcoming wedding?

Success!!

From there, it started to snowball. I told the NYU students that if they could give kits to reporters and bring back their business cards, I'd throw a $10 bounty at them per card. That got them started; they made it a contest to seek out and find media all over the convention.

For the remaining two days of the convention, we had the NYU students working overtime. They were outside from 7 A.M. to 8 P.M., handing out kits. People who knew how to knit immediately started knitting in the car, while waiting in bumper-to-bumper traffic. We watched people in traffic who didn't know how to knit look at them, laugh, and put them on the seat next to them.

We even had a few people call over the NYU kids to their cars, and tell them that their wives loved the yarn so much, they wanted another sample, to hold them over until the weekend so the family could go to Flying Fingers together and buy much more of it. Truly amazing.

A few reporters started calling me on my mobile phone, having gotten the number from the students who gave them kits. We got Flying Fingers a few fun mentions in various papers both in New York City, as well as other places in the country. Remember, all the media in the world was in town covering the convention.

?!?!?!?!?!?!?!?!?

> **Rule:** If you tie a promotion or stunt into an event currently going on, you can secure all the media that's already there. It's about timeliness.

For weeks after the convention ended, people were still walking into the store with their kits, asking to buy more yarn. They were calling the store, ordering over the phone.

Elise said it was the largest one-month surge they'd ever had. We wound up breaking that record a few months later, but for the time being, Flying Fingers was indeed flying high.

Now it was time to top ourselves.

Elise and Kevin's biggest complaint was that people from New York City never came to their store. They'd heard about Flying Fingers, people knew of them, but to actually get New York City people to leave the nest and go "upstate" (even though it was a mere 21 miles away), was a harder challenge than trying to get me to learn to knit.

When we talked to knitters in Manhattan, we asked them if they'd ever heard of Flying Fingers, and if they would consider going to the store. When we mentioned the different types of yarn FFYS had, and how no one else had them, they were ecstatic. But then they realized where it was, and they tended to give one of two responses:

1. "Oh, it's outside the city? I don't have a car."
2. "I'd have to take a *train?*"

Needless to say, the idea of going out of the city for yarn wasn't too appealing for anybody. There's just something about leaving the confines of New York City that scares most people. Maybe it's the abundance of trees, or lack of tall buildings.

So after much research, after interviewing hundreds of knitters in New York City, and after frequent attempts at learning how to knit, we decided that the only way to get New Yorkers to go to Flying Fingers Yarn Shop in Irvington, NY, was to take them ourselves.

But how? We weren't operating a shuttle service! Flying Fingers was a yarn store! That was their business, not driving people to their store from midtown.

We threw ideas around for a few days in our office. Rent a cab. Hire a car service one day a week. Buy a limo . . . but nothing seemed to help convey the sense of yarn, or knitting, or the cool and wacky style of the store itself, no matter what we came up with.

Then, the magic happened. . . .

"Wouldn't it be funny," I thought, "if we had rocket-powered knitting needles. You sat on them, like broomsticks, and they took you right to Flying Fingers."

"Or perhaps giant balls of yarn that people could follow to get to the store."

"Well, actually, what if the giant balls of yarn were attached to something, like signs, or something, that showed people the way?"

"No, what we need is some kind of car with big knitting needles that says, 'Follow me to Flying Fingers!'"

"A YARN BUS!"

"A what?"

"A YARN BUS! A giant bus that drives people from the city to Flying Fingers and back! With giant balls of yarn and knitting needles all over it! Like a shuttle! Like the Oscar Meyer Weiner-Mobile!"

We all looked at each other, in fits of giggles. We knew we'd hit on a winner. We imagined the giant yarn bus, driving through Manhattan, picking people up, taking them to Flying Fingers. We imagined people stopped in their cars, staring, mouths agape, as this giant ball of yarn with needles sticking out of the top drove on by.

Now, we just had to sell it.

?!?!?!?!?!?!?!?

> **Rule: When the brilliant idea finally materializes, you can't stop it; it's like trying to stop a tidal wave. All you can do is grab a pen, write it down, and try not to laugh.**

As it turns out, selling the Yarn Bus to Kevin and Elise was easy—they loved the idea. They couldn't stop laughing! The real question was, how long would it take to build, and who would build it? How do you get a 16-passenger van converted into a "Yarn Bus" in a short amount of time? Is it even doable?

Well, as it turns out, the people who built the Oscar Meyer Weiner-Mobile, a company named Prototype Source out of California, had some free time on their hands. We called some guys in Connecticut we knew who designed a garbage truck for Yoo-hoo Chocolate Drink, called Bochanis Rogan Zoom, and between the two of them and us, managed to get a Yarn Bus built, shipped, and delivered to Flying Fingers in about five months.

And then, the magic started to happen.

I remember the day it showed up—we'd been actively pitching the story to the media, and both the New York *Daily News* and *New York Post* had agreed to run items about it without a photo—a major coup for us, as it gave us credibility. It also gave us a headache, though, as we committed to a date that the bus would start making pickups—and we didn't know if we could even get the bus by that time.

Multiple calls, frantic emails, and finally, several cell phone conversations later, the two college kids, who we hired to drive the bus back from the West Coast where it was built, delivered the Yarn Bus into midtown Manhattan. I was on the corner when it turned onto 6th Avenue, and I'll tell you . . . even though I'd seen photos of it during construction, and knew what it was going to look like, it was still a sight to behold. It was massive. It was a giant van, with yarn and knitting needles! It was the most amazing thing!

And it was ours. (See Figure 5.1.)

The first second it came down the street, we knew we had something special. I'd talked the local ABC affiliate into doing a segment that night on the news, welcoming the Yarn Bus to New York. As the bus rolled up 6th Avenue and pulled in front of the camera crews, I heard the cameraman say, "How cool," and I knew we had a winner.

We posted the bus schedule on the website, and people started signing up for the free ride.

The media had a field day with the story, as you might expect. It's not often you're driving up the West Side Highway and happen to see three giant balls of yarn in the next lane.

Figure 5.1   The Yarn Bus.

ABC News, CBS, Fox, they all loved it. The *New Yorker* did a three-page story entitled "In Stitches: From Here to There Department," with a first person account of taking a ride on the Yarn Bus.

Martha Stewart led off the second taping of her new talk show by driving the Yarn Bus to the studio for "Poncho Day."

Really, really great press.

We put hundreds of flyers in the van, because we found that whenever we'd stop at a red light, or a stop sign, or in traffic, people would roll down their windows and ask us what we were doing. So we created flyers that told them where our store was, how to get to it, what our website was, and the like.

Then, we started doing something we thought might help. . . .

We started going after blogs.

We noticed that it seemed that for every knitter out there who knew how to use a computer, there was a blog about what they were knitting.

Quick, five-second blog primer: A blog is sort of an updated online diary. There are millions of blogs out there, covering every conceivable topic in the world. People update them when they feel like it, anywhere from every hour to once a week or longer. Blogs have really taken off in the past three years, and as of September 2006, Technorati (a blog search engine at www.technorati.com) reported close to 55,300,000 blogs, but most estimates say there are many, many more than that. For more places to learn about blogs, see the Resources chapter.

So we quickly became knitting blog experts. We found out which blogs were active, what people were talking about, and which blogs were considered authoritative on the subject of all things knitting.

We did it however, not in a PR-type way, but rather, in a straightforward, "here's who we are and what we want" way.

We'd email the writers of the blogs and be straight up with them:

Hi there. We're aware that <blog name here> is one of the more influential knitting blogs out there, so we thought we'd share this bit of info with you. Feel free to use it, if you'd like. We're working with a company called Flying Fingers Yarn Shop. They just launched this really cool Yarn Bus, and are driving it back and forth from Manhattan to their store in Irvington, NY, a few times a week, picking up customers and bringing them back. We thought you'd want to know because we're sure you have readers from New York, and also, take a look at the photo, it's a really cool bus! Anyhow, if you want more info, feel free to email me. Thanks so much!

And that was it. We enclosed a little photo of the Yarn Bus, and waited.

Sure enough, we started getting emails from blog writers. They loved the bus, and loved the concept behind it! A lot of blogs posted links to Flying Fingers' website, and online sales increased as well. In addition, a lot of blogs started talking about organizing trips to New York to try and catch a ride on the bus.

Of course, we got the occasional, "Stop telling me how to write my blog!" emails from people, as well, but we kindly replied that we were doing no such thing. We politely tried to assure that we were just trying to offer a new bit of information to them. You'll always get one or two replies like that, whether you're pitching to a blogger or to the *New York Times*. Pitching the right way and going back and rereading Chapter 2 will help to drastically cut down on the number of "go away" emails you receive.

The vast majority of blog writers, however, loved the Yarn Bus, and gave it tons of coverage. Business increased both online and at the store, and the store was generating a lot of revenue from the bus.

The store started getting calls from people in other states, asking how many people they'd need to bring to the store to convince Kevin and Elise to drive the bus to their state and pick them up. It got to the point where we had to issue a "mileage rule." We couldn't allow the bus to pick up groups over 300 miles away, except under special circumstances. Of course, this doesn't stop people from emailing and asking, and on occasion, the bus gets sent out on missions to states up and down the East Coast.

?!?!?!?!?!?!?!?

> **Rule:** Blogs are just like any other media. Keep your pitch on target, on message, short, and to the point. If the writer is interested, they'll either email you back, or post outright. Be aware, though, there's much less of a fact-checking process on some blogs. Although they'll try to be accurate, they don't necessarily have fact-checking departments for everything they post.

As the bus continued to gain notoriety and more people got a chance to ride in it, Flying Fingers had a new problem on their hands. They needed to hire someone new to drive the bus! Their current driver was moving and without a driver, the bus was nothing more than art on wheels.

Never being an agency to miss turning anything into a media opportunity, we realized that this was a perfect chance to score some additional press, if not with the mainstream media, then with the blogs and websites. So we did what anyone does when trying to hire someone: We issued a call, in the form of an email, for a driver:

?!

Dear All:

A very, very cool job opportunity exists with one of my clients.

Flying Fingers Yarn Shop, in Irvington, NY (21 miles from Manhattan) is quickly becoming the largest yarn store not ONLY on the East Coast, but in the entire country. You can get a look at them at www.flyingfingers.com.

About a year ago, we helped them create a super cool way for people from Manhattan to shop their wares.

Six months later, the Yarn Bus was born.

This is the famed Yarn Bus that has been covered in countless media around the globe. It's well known in knitting circles, and is quickly becoming one of the coolest promotions we've ever been involved with for any client.

The Yarn bus makes the trip from NYC to Irvington twice on Saturdays and Sundays, and occasionally during the week. It also makes special appearances at news events and the like.

This bus was designed by the same people who built the Oscar Meyer Weiner-Mobile and the Yoo-hoo Stinkin' Summer Tour Garbage Truck. It's a blast to drive, and you don't need any special kind of license.

Flying Fingers is looking for a driver for the bus—someone who likes to have fun, but is responsible, and won't try to pull an Otto from the Simpsons on the bus. There will also be some helping out in the store, as well. If you don't know how to knit, trust me, you will by the time you take your next job.

The pay is $15 per hour, which, by the way, is what school-bus drivers make—so they're competitive. Plus, you'll get all the free yarn, knitting needles, and knitting classes you could ever want.

If you're interested, send me an interesting cover letter, telling me why you'd be the perfect Yarn Bus driver. Enclose your resume, as well, either as a Word doc or a pdf.

Feel free to pass this around to all your friends—in fact, I'd appreciate it!

Oh, and one other thing—make sure you're comfortable being on TV and in the news—because you will be.

—Peter

?!

We sent it out to everyone, and it got forwarded around like wildfire. Flying Fingers received hundreds of resumes, and actually had a pretty hard time choosing a final candidate. The amount of pickup it got on the web drove even more traffic to the website. By putting in not only the store website, but a link to the bus, it made the story much more visual, and allowed people to visit the site right from their email. This helped give an "identity" to the store, and even brought more buyers in.

?!?!?!?!?!?!?!

Rule: We've said this before: Everything should be a potential media opportunity. Look at everything as a chance to get more media and more exposure for your client. A job offer, a request for hire, anything—it can all be a potential media opportunity, if you play it right. You don't have to turn it into some giant story with press releases and requests for coverage, just make sure you get what you're trying to do to the right people, in a short, concise way. If you've figured out how to make it newsworthy, it'll get picked up.

So what's the end result here? For Flying Fingers, they got their name squarely onto the map. They were doing well, now they're doing super-well. Their business has increased by leaps and bounds. People are still lining up to get a ride on the Yarn Bus. They're known for it. They've also become known for selling amazing yarns, and the media calls them whenever they're doing a story on knitting.

As an added bonus, every weekend, hundreds of people do double-takes as they're driving down the street, and they're passed by three giant balls of multi-colored yarn.

T A K E - A W A Y S

WHAT WE LEARNED
FROM THIS CHAPTER

1. Always call back right away. Always take the meeting.

2. You never know where the next big client is going to come from. Always go in with an open mind—never judge a book by its cover.

3. The brainstorming will produce the most insane ideas when you least expect them. Be ready to write them down and act on them super-fast.

4. Timeliness matters: come up with stunts and ideas that fit into the timeline of what's going on in the world. It allows you to work with the press that's already there, and if there's a correlation, allows the press to get two stories out of the event, instead of just one.

5. Go big or go home: even without a huge budget, you can create ideas that will stick in people's minds—the key is to work with ideas that will not only promote the company or client once, but on a daily basis. In our case, the Yarn Bus does its job every time it picks up a customer.

CHAPTER 6

?I?I?I?I?I?I?I?I?I?I?I?I?I?I?I?I?I?I?I?I?I?I?I?I?I?I?I?I?I?I?I?I?I?I?I?I?I?I?I?I?I?I?I?I?I?I?I?I?I?I?I?I?I?I

Coming Up with and Implementing the Big Idea—Part Three

THE WEBSITE THAT LAUNCHED 20,000 PLANES . . . AND COUNTING.

Ask any publicist who has been online since the typewriter was the main source of communication (i.e., pre-1991). They'll tell you that pitching media about anything having to do with on-line was a lot easier in the old days. Why? Because the Internet was brand new!

"We've got a website."

"They've got a website! Check it out! It's a website! It has a moving picture that goes back and forth. Look—an envelope where you can send them an email! This is incredible! This is front-page news!"

Ah, the good old days.

I remember the Internet trade shows back in the mid-1990s, both as a consumer and attendee, as well as a consultant to the exhibiting companies. It was insane. We'd work 15 to 18-hour days, then rush back to the hotel, change, and go from party to party to party, which were being sponsored by the next great Internet company.

Well, we all know what happened then.

But . . . we don't necessarily realize that something else happened in the Internet world, as well. Once the great shakeout was over, the companies that survived generally became just like any other company. They had a presence (a website, in this case), they sold a product (either a physical product or a service or advertising), and they either made or lost money.

In other words, the great "WOW! YOU'VE GOT A WEBSITE!" hype that got tons of companies tons of ink died right along with the Pets.com sock puppet.

Naturally, two immediate schools of thought come into play here. The first one (and the one to which the majority of us subscribe) states that the less those "ankle-biter" companies get press, the more room there is for companies with an actual *story* to tell. This is important. Reporters, as we've discussed over and over, only have a finite number of hours in their day, inches in their column, memory on their hard drive, whatever. They have to make decisions based on what they consider to be newsworthy. If you have no story, you're not newsworthy. Like I said, this is a good thing for those of us with actual stories to tell.

The second school of thought goes something like this: "OH NO, WE ACTUALLY HAVE TO HAVE A STORY ON WHAT CAN WE DO?" Repeat this a thousand times in a thousand different ways (i.e., "Repainting the conference room is not a newsworthy story," or "No one outside this company, and especially not the *New York Times,* cares that you landed a $6,000 account this morning"), and you've got the battle cry of the clueless–"But then how do we get coverage?" This is the oft-heard scream of a CEO with one too many people kissing his butt and telling him how great he is to the point where he starts to believe it.

Now of course, if we eventually wind up in the dotcom boom Part II, then none of this will matter, and you can pitch with reckless abandon the news that your whole office just bought personalized Razor Scooters.

Assuming, however, that doesn't happen, this chapter is sort of a primer on how to take an idea that hasn't before existed, create it, spin it, and get the media's attention for it.

SO YOU'VE GOT A BIG IDEA

> **Rule:** Got a big idea? Want to tell the world? First thing to do? Shut up. Hammer out the details. You get one chance to make a first impression. Want coverage? Make that first impression count.

You know the great joke: Guy comes home and says, "Honey, I've got the greatest idea–we're gonna make a fortune. We'll sell one-dollar-bills for ninety-nine cents! It can't miss!"

Wife says, "Are you crazy? We'll lose money on every sale! We'll be broke!"

Guy retorts, "Don't worry. We'll make it up in volume."

Applied to the PR industry, that could be read the same way. If you can't answer any and every possible question that the media could potentially throw at you, then you're not ready to speak to the media. Have your ducks in a row. Always.

So the idea came to me on a plane. As I've said, I travel a lot for work; 99.9 percent of the time, I'm sitting next to Joe No-Shower, or Jill Never-Shut-Up. It's sort of a given, it's one of the downsides of travel. It happens. You deal with it; it's what they make noise-cancelling headphones for.

But one day, who sits down next to me but Ms. Texas, 2002. I remember looking up from my book, and going speechless. For me, as a publicist, that's a rarity. I remember thinking, "Hmmm. This doesn't suck."

The next four hours of the flight were a blur, and the next thing I remember was landing at Newark.

Later, when I analyzed the flight, I tried to think about why it went so fast–it certainly wasn't the airline food. Obviously, it was the company. No, we didn't fall in love and get married over Cleveland–we just had a really lovely conversation, some really interesting talk, and it made the trip go by a lot faster. One could say it made it painless, in fact.

Of course, in my little balanced world, two days later, I was flying from New York to Boston, and wound up sitting next to a couple from Boca, who spent the entire trip screaming at me in heavily accented voices about why I'd be perfect for their daughter. They just *had* to set me up with her. It got to the point where I agreed simply to get them to stop talking. Of course, that only prompted them to talk more–what she was like, what she was looking for in a husband (eeek!), and other fun facts about which I simply could not have cared less.

So, I put two and two together. Why did my four-hour flight take seven seconds, and my 45-minute flight take several ice ages?

The answer, obviously, was because of my seatmate.

It occurred to me that we have control over every other aspect of our flight. Where we want to go. When we want to go. Which day. How we want to get there. A direct flight or one that makes stops.

And then, because as I've mentioned, I'm severely ADHD, I forgot about it.

Until I had a string of bad seatmates in a row. Then I thought, OK, maybe it's time to see what I can do.

A year (and much secret-ness later) AirTroductions.com was born.

The concept is simple: Build a profile, enter your flight information, and it shows you who else is on your flight, based on other people who've voluntarily entered their info, as well.

It's almost too simple. It smacks of "why-hasn't-anyone-else-thought-of-this-before?"

?!?!?!?!?!?!?!?

Rule: (This applies not only to PR and marketing, but life in general.) If your first thought is, "This is too simple; why hasn't anyone else thought of this before?" then that leads to three possible conclusions: (1) Someone has, and you just haven't heard about it; (2) Someone has, and they're doing a terrible job of marketing it; or (3) It really doesn't exist, and you're the luckiest person in the world.

So there I was, with this handy-dandy, spiffy new website built, and now I just had to get the word out.

Piece of cake, right?

Hardly.

I thought I scored a major, major coup, when I told a reporter friend from *Fortune* about my idea. He called me a few days later with the news all publicists love to hear: "My editor is interested."

I remember chatting with a friend of mine the night before the magazine was supposed to come out. It went something like this:

Me: "Do you know how many people read *Fortune*? And they're all business travelers! This is gonna rock! Everyone's gonna read it, and sign up, and oh, man! This will be amazing!"

Him: "Perhaps."

Me: "What do you mean, perhaps? This is gonna rock!"

Him: "Hopefully."

Me: "Shut up."

Thinking back on it, I was being just like the classic pain-in-the-butt client: I wasn't listening. I was sure that my way was the best way, and I was not giving a second to even remotely entertain the possibility that I might not know every little thing.

And so the article ran, and Monday morning found me sitting at my computer, staring anxiously at the counter on the site, waiting for the numbers to go up, up, up!

And I sat. And sat.

And my butt started to go numb.

And the numbers went up.

By one. Or two.

And I sat.

Finally, it occurred to me that *Fortune* magazine wasn't going to provide the giant, massive membership boom I had predicted the night before.

Of course, I realized this little gem of a fact after I'd told a handful of friends to "check the website and see our numbers tomorrow!"

Classic.

> **Rule:** The press isn't finished until after it goes into print. And even then, don't make bets using the media as collateral. It'll come back to bite you.

Back to our story. I read and re-read the *Fortune* article. I simply couldn't for the life of me figure out why it wasn't working! It was a great piece, virtually entirely positive. Everyone was quoted well. It ran in a prominent section of the magazine. It should have been mega-huge! Everyone should have been reading this at their offices, on their airplanes, in their taxis, in bed, at their gyms, wherever, and signing right up! I just flat-out didn't get it!

Then, a friend of mine called. In 18 words, he summed up the answer to my confusion.

"Hmm . . . I wonder if people are going to remember to go to the site after reading the article?"

It hit me like a ton of laptops, and it made perfect sense: Mine was a company that lent itself to great press, but didn't have an immediacy to it.

> **Rule:** Know your company, and know what kind of media will do what for it. If you're an online company, make sure you either (1) have an immediacy to your company, or (2) have a way to get people there. Reading an article about your company while on the subway is great, but will the reader remember to type in the URL when they get home?
>
> **Example:** If you have a company that is doing some sort of stunt or event on Thursday, that's an immediacy. That's the lead you want to get to the media, and want the media to cover. The logic there is, "I'm reading about this on a Tuesday. I have to act before Thursday. If I don't, I'm screwed."

Because the *Fortune* article had no immediacy to it, it was treated as such. It became an, "Oh, that's a cool idea. I'll have to remember to try that" story, and it was, in most cases, filed by business travelers, and quickly forgotten.

My concept was simple: reach the people who travel the most and tell them about this service. They'd love it, sign up, and I'd make a million.

Yes, in theory.

Problem was, I was relying on them to remember their last flight and the last time they had to sit next to nonbathing-man. The readers of *Fortune*, mostly, were not. They were on the commuter railroad. Or in their office. Or at the gym. Or in the spa. The chances of them reading this article on the plane, when they were next to nonbathing-man, were slim. In other words, I was hoping for a call-to-action that many of them simply didn't feel.

It was a valuable lesson.

BUT . . . under the "valuable lesson with a nice twist" category, I remembered that the media reads other media, too.

In other words, the reporter from *USA Today* reads *Fortune*. As does the reporter from *BusinessWeek*. And the *Los Angeles Times*. And *Newsweek*. And *People* . . . etc., etc., etc.

And the calls started coming in from the media. They weren't the thousands of new members I'd hoped for but slowly, the calls started coming in.

An article in *USA Today* brought another four hundred members.

A one-paragraph blurb in *BusinessWeek* kicked in a few hundred, too.

Then the phone rang, and it was the production company for the Lisa Loeb Reality TV Show, *#1 Single*. She was flying to New York in an upcoming episode, and would it be OK if she used the site to try and get a date on the show?

You've never heard someone say "yes" so fast in your life.

> **Rule: If someone bigger calls and offers you a chance to latch onto their coattails, free of charge, with no hidden agenda, DO IT.**

Ok. We had that placement coming up. Of course, that wasn't going to hit for about three months or so, so we had to still keep busy.

Little by little, the media started to figure it out. We were telling everyone we knew—emailing travel reporters (with a very basic pitch, two paragraphs) explaining that we'd found a cure for "Airplane Not-Next-to-Me-Itis" and offering them a free press account.

Reporters, as I mentioned, travel a lot. As such, they quickly got the concept—they've all been there. And because they were media, and saw the potential for a story, they all signed up. They didn't need the call to action that the general public needed; they "got it" right away.

?!?!?!?!?!?!?!?

> **Rule:** Media tends to be much savvier than the general public. Use this to your advantage. If they have a *compelling* reason to check something out, they usually will. Compelling of course, means short, to the point, with a purpose, and a target that relates to them.

In other words, I was pitching AirTroductions to media that mattered: business, financial, and of course, travel.

Little by little, the momentum hit. The *New York Post* ran a spectacular story touting AirTroductions as the next big dating site. A number of radio stations started talking about "love in the air." And several local market TV stations did stories on their own from local airports, interviewing people and asking them, "Do you think you could find love in the sky?"

While I was enjoying all the press, my next thought was, "Wait a second! This isn't only a dating site! It's a networking site, too! People can use this site to meet other people for lots of reasons, not just for dating! Wait!"

But, the media had spoken.

Ever try to get the toothpaste back in the tube? Never works, and gets all over everything. Toothpaste was quickly taking up residence all over my office.

?!?!?!?!?!?!?!?

> **Rule:** Is your company clearly defined? If not, is the potential for misunder-standing there? And if it is, what are you doing to correct it? Or, is it already too late?
>
> **Corollary to that rule:** Are you adaptable?

AirTroductions is adaptable, fortunately. It was interesting, though, watching us change. We didn't "do" anything, per se, to the site, but we changed the way we spoke about it. All of a sudden, it wasn't a "networking site on the airplane," but a "way to choose your seatmate for networking, friendship, or anything in between!" It was no longer "a way to close the deal in the sky," but rather, "a way to avoid the psychological drama that comes from sitting two inches away from someone you don't know for eight hours at a time."

And the media "got" that even quicker than the networking story.

"Love is in the air! We love it! Let's run with it!" was the most common response we got back.

And hey, if that's what the mainstream press wanted to hear, we were happy to oblige. It let us go after business press with one pitch, consumer press with another, and never the twain shall meet.

But we still weren't getting massive numbers.

Until American Airlines inflight magazine, *American Way*, published a story on us, complete with a cover teaser: "Could Your Seatmate be Your Soul Mate?"

That story came out in their January edition, and hit plane seatbacks January 1. By January 2, we'd increased our numbers by 1,000. By the end of January, we were up by over 5,000 new members.

The most valuable lesson of AirTroductions' short life to date:

?!?!?!?!?!?!?!?

> **Rule:** Hit 'em where they are.
>
> **Corollary to that rule:** "Hit 'em where they ain't" only works in baseball.

Why the sudden burst? The answer was obvious: people who were being forced to sit next to annoying people were reading an article about how not to have to sit next to an annoying person! It was insanity, and perfectly timed.

Because what hit the TV airwaves in late January?

Lisa Loeb.

> **Rule:** Have some way of knowing what's going on with your company, be it a mobile phone, email alerts, or whatever works for you. But be religious about staying in touch.

The scene: Dinner with mom and dad, a local restaurant halfway between their apartment and my apartment.

The time: Around 9 P.M., Sunday night.

The meal: Fish, I think.

My mobile phone goes off, and I look at it. It's my friend Michael, who works the site for me, approving profiles, keeping an eye on it.

"Peter, did we have a news story or something break today?"

"No, why?"

"We're seeing quite the number of new members."

"What's 'quite the number' mean?"

"Well, over 500 in the past 20 minutes."

Blink.

I pulled out my Blackberry, and entered the unlock code. It took several seconds to process–always a bad (or good, depending on how you look at it) sign, meaning its little CPU was a bit busy doing other things. Like downloading over 750 emails.

New Messages: 847.

Messages from ADMIN@AIRTRODUCTIONS.COM: 817.

"Um, mom and dad? Uh . . . can I wrap up my fish to go? I think I need to get into the office."

Lisa Loeb's reality show had premiered, and she'd used AirTroductions to fly across the country.

The way I'd expected it, she'd use it as "a dating service," and maybe the site would get a quick name mention, and they'd move on.

What actually happened:

Lisa says, "Hey, I heard about this new site called AirTroductions that lets you get a date on an airplane! I want to try it!"

Cut to more than ONE FULL MINUTE (Seriously! More than 60 seconds!) of her entering in her profile, seeing who was on her flight, and actually chatting online with him, complete with over 30 seconds of screen shots of the website.

I was beyond floored.

> **Rule: Don't expect. Plan. You never know how something is going to be played. And it could be the best play of your life.**

Racing to my office, I called three friends on the West Coast, where the show had yet to air–"You've got to tape *#1 Single* for me!" They all acted like I was insane, until I explained why.

Upon arriving, sure enough, we had well over a thousand new members, and the numbers were increasing by the minute. It was again, insanity. I never thought anything would come from a reality show–hadn't they peaked? Apparently not. We were literally getting close to two new members a minute, for well over an hour each time the show premiered in each time zone!

And we learned a valuable lesson that day, too. Reality shows, especially on cable, are shown over and over and over and over again. This continues to make me quite happy.

> **Rule: Never turn down the possible promotion. You never know where it'll wind you up. This applies to journalists, too. Never turn down the interview. Never turn down the reporter's request. It might be a small paper, but people read small papers. That cub reporter at the local weekly could be tomorrow's Page 1 editor at the *Washington Post*.**

And besides, if you've read ANYTHING I've written for the past 97 pages, you know—it's all about Karma.

Over the next week or so, things started to trickle back down to normal. New members every day, but at a manageable pace. It was good, and we were thinking about the next big press release, what would we announce, and where we would announce it.

We never got the chance.

> **Rule:** If you can help it, never let phone calls from unrecognized numbers go to voice mail. You never know who might be on the other end.

"Hi, this is Peter!"

"Hi, this is Ellen Wulfhorst, correspondent at Reuters in New York. I'd like to do a story on AirTroductions. Are you available for a chat?"

> **Rule:** When anyone from a major wire service calls you and asks if you're available for a chat, it does not matter what you're doing. You could very well have six supermodels lined up outside your door, all waiting to do your bidding; it's irrelevant. YOU ARE AVAILABLE FOR A CHAT. We're clear on this point, yes?

Ellen immediately got the concept—she's one of the smartest reporters in the field today, I believe. She knew why the site was started, and asked very probing, detailed questions.

She interviewed me, a number of members, and interviewed some other people in the industry. One of them wasn't so positive on the concept, but he was quickly drowned out by those who were. I hated knowing that someone out there didn't like my idea, my baby, as it were, but, as Gordon Gekko said in the movie *Wall Street*, it's business. Never personal. Or maybe that was Ice-T in *New Jack City*. Either way, it's true. You can't please all of the people all of the time.

Besides, end result—over 6,000 new members from that story, and the subsequent media that came from it, including *Good Morning America,* CNN, and CNBC.

So now what?

?!?!?!?!?!?!?!?

Rule: You can rest when you're dead.

We managed to get some really nice press for AirTroductions in the first four months of existence. But now what? Well, we issued a release when we broke 10,000 members; that put a few more pins in the map.

The key for us, though, is continued exposure. We need to keep AirTroductions in the forefront of travelers' minds; if they're traveling, we want them to know about AirTroductions. So how to we do that?

Well, remember a few chapters ago, how we talked about expert positioning and how it works? How if you've got no hard news, position yourself as an expert?

Remember the good Karma email?

Tie the two together, and what do you have?

An expert who knows everything about business and personal travel, and is willing to be quoted on a moment's notice.

?!

Dear Travel Reporter (and yes, I used each person's name):
(Quick, four-second email)

I'm not pitching you, just offering myself up as a source. I travel approximately 250,000 miles per year, and spend the majority of my time on a plane, somewhere over the globe. Because of this, it occurred to me to launch a company that allows members to choose who they sit next to, as opposed to just where they sit. (The site is called AirTroductions. If you desire to check it out, it's at www.airtroductions.com.)

But, the reason I'm emailing is just to offer myself as a source. I know tons of people in the travel industry, plus, as much as I travel, I have some great anecdotes myself. So if you ever find yourself on deadline, feel free to call—I can probably help, or find someone who can.

All the best,

—Peter Shankman
peter@airtroductions.com

?!

Simple and to the point. Lets the reporter or editor know the following: (1) I'm not pitching them for a story; (2) I'm not wasting their time; and (3) I'm available to make their lives easier when they're on deadline.

Know what the number one reply was that I got back most often from that email?

"Wait, you created a company that lets people choose WHO they sit next to? Tell me more about that!"

Sounds good to me! Reporter was thrilled to "discover" something, I was thrilled for the exposure for AirTroductions–it was a win/win.

Again, the key is simplicity. How can I make the reporter's life easier, while helping my cause at the same time?

As the site continues to grow, we get the random "out of the blue" reporter emailing and saying, "Hey, we'd like to do a story on AirTroductions. Can you find us some people in <insert town where media is based> who would be willing to talk?"

That's always tricky. We value our members above all else, and never give out information without explicit consent first.

?!?!?!?!?!?!?!?

> **Rule:** Your members (clients, advertisers, etc.) pay the bills. Treat them with utmost respect. (Always.)
>
> **Another Rule:** If you do treat them with respect, though, there's no reason you can't put them to work for you. You'll find that for small tokens of appreciation, they'll gladly become your biggest fans.

For instance, a reporter called us recently from the *Chicago Tribune.* He was writing an article. Who did we know who could talk about how they're using AirTroductions?

We're based in New York. Who DID we know? Not many people.

We called a few, got one possible lead. Great. Then, we turned it over to our members, and posted this on the front page of the site:

> 5/8/2006 URGENT! If you're flying through CHICAGO (any airport) either TODAY or TOMORROW (5/8 or 5/9), a reporter with a major Chicago newspaper wants to take your picture and we'll give you FREE AIRTRODUCTIONS FOR LIFE. Email success@airtroductions.com ASAP if this is you!

Guess what happened? Ten emails in 4 hours from AirTroductions members. We got two of them in touch with the reporter, and they got free memberships. Didn't cost us any hard currency, and now they're telling all their friends about it. And you know the conversation is going to go something like this:

Our Member: "Oh my God! You've got to buy the *Chicago Tribune* on Thursday! I'm totally going to be in it!"

Member's friend: "Why?"

Our Member: "There's this website I use when I travel that lets me choose my seatmate, and they're writing about it and they're going to use me and they gave me a free membership and . . ."

Member's friend: "Wait, you can choose who you sit next to? What's the site?"

Boom. New member.

?!?!?!?!?!?!?!?

Rule: Your clients, members, etc. *WANT* to work for you! Remind them of that! Give them something fun to get out of it, and they'll love you forever.

(continued)

?!?!?!?!?!?!?!?!?

> Give them something really fun, and they'll scream their heads off about how great and wonderful you are. Put them in the paper, and they'll have your children.

Finally, let's talk for a second about continuing the process. Ok, we're getting press. We've sort of gotten into a rut here. How do we break out of it and regain that same excitement we had when we first started?

It happens to the best of us. You get a great hit—the Reuters piece, *Good Morning America,* you name it. Next thing you know, you're basking in the glory of a great hit, and all of a sudden, your middle name changes to complacency, and you're wondering why you haven't had a hit in 20 days.

Here's how to prevent that.

Peter's Top Five Rules to Avoiding PR Complacency

5. Have you really exhausted every conceivable possibility for publicity without crossing over the "this has nothing to do with my beat" line? Go research five reporters in your industry and see what they covered six months ago. Figure out a tie-in.

4. Who else is in your space, doing what you or your clients do? How about pitching a round-up article? Sure, it's not as good as a solo, but it's better than not having anything. If you're in competition, how about a shoot-out? Offer the reporter free access, a journalist copy or piece of whatever it is you do/make/produce, and tell him to ask other companies in your space for the same for a comparison piece.

3. Talk to your members/clients/their clients . . . what are they doing that's new? How are they using you or your client? What are they doing that's exciting? Are they doing it in a different way? Offer them goodies to talk.

2. Hungry? How about a gathering, over food, of the top leaders in your space? A lively debate about the future of your in-

dustry is sure to bring out the best journalists who cover you. Much like the reason people go to NASCAR, they want to see a nasty crash with blood.

1. And the number one way to avoid complacency–put it aside. Close the books. Go for a run. Take a walk. Come back refreshed, with a bunch of new ideas and different ways of thinking. Then use those to your advantage. They do work. I swear.

Whatever you do, don't give up. Don't rest on your laurels. Don't think, "Oh, we got *Good Morning America*. That'll hold us for a while." Because you know what? It won't. What it will do is rev up your competitors. Think about how you feel when a competitor lands a great media hit and you're shut out. Chaps your hide, makes you work ten times as hard, right? Same thing happens on the flip side. Do you want to be there, smiling and being all "Yup, look what I got," while a competitor passes you doing 110 and you look like you're standing still?

I didn't think so.

WHAT WE LEARNED
FROM THIS CHAPTER

1. When the big idea strikes, be quiet until you can answer every question perfectly, or at least until you have some idea of what you're going to say.

2. Make sure you don't expect one piece of media to skyrocket you to fame. Sure, it seems like that's how it happens, but believe me—it doesn't. It's consistent, repeated stories in publications all around the spectrum, over and over, that lead to good press.

3. Have a call to action. The article is great, but if people don't remember to follow up with it, what's the point? Either fashion a date/time call to action, or position the piece somewhere where people will immediately "get it" (i.e., trapped in an airplane with a smelly man sitting next to them).

4. Always have a way of being contacted. If the story runs and the dam breaks and you're flooded with members, orders, or the like, you want to be there. Not an assistant, not a junior person. You. This is your moment. Shine.

5. You're never too busy to take the meeting or answer the phone for the unknown number. You

never know where the next monster story will come from.

6. Don't relax too soon. One major hit does not retirement make.

?!

CHAPTER 7

Coming Up with and Implementing the Big Idea and What Happens When It's Too Successful?

HOW TO SHUT DOWN THE INTERNET FOR A NIGHT USING ONE PR STUNT

"Be careful what you wish for, you just might get it," says the old adage. That's true in all aspects of life, but perhaps never more so than in public relations.

We all think about the "great stunt." Wow, wouldn't it be awesome if we could just do <insert amazing idea here>. Ninety-nine percent of the time, it rolls around in the bowl of tapioca we call our brain, secure in the knowledge that no client in their right mind would ever approve it.

"Yeah, let's create a giant 75-foot tall bowl of JELL-O and host diving competitions," we say, knowing full well we'll never even have to do the most basic of spec-work on an idea like that.

But occasionally, that backfires. You're going to want to keep a few bottles of antacids around for when that happens. Trust me.

In rare cases, the client will say "Hey, that sounds like a good idea—let's do it!" Don't panic. I'm going to show you how it can be done.

First, a little background.

My firm, The Geek Factory, was contacted back in the dot-com heyday to help promote a domain name registration firm. They were small, and at the time, no one had heard of them. They found us, like all of our clients, through word of mouth.

"We have this idea that domain name registration shouldn't cost $70 per name," they said, when we met them for the first time. Keep in mind, back in those days, that's how much it cost to register a domain name–$70 per name, for a number of years. A bunch of other companies came around and the price dropped, and now, you can get it for almost nothing. But back then, it was $70 minimum.

"So what we want you to do is to write a press release saying that we're the cheapest, and put it on the newswire. That should bring everyone to us."

But if you've read so much as ONE PAGE of this book, you know darn well that the above recipe is nothing but a one-way ticket to no-press-ville.

Of course, we told them that. We said we'd come up with a few better (we called them "different") ideas, and get back to them.

In brainstorming, we came across the typical problem for most start-up Internet companies: this was an online company. What exciting guerilla-type event could we do that would not only get noticed, but also tie into the product?

?!?!?!?!?!?!?!?!?

> **Rule: A guerilla event is only good if it *not only* gets attention, but ties the user *right* back to the brand. Without that, it's just a stunt for stunt's sake. And that's more or less pointless.**

So we started brainstorming. What was a domain name, anyway? Well, it was a pointer. Something that told someone where to go online, as opposed to saying, "Go to http://219.34 .945.011." It made it a little more user-friendly.

The first question that came to mind was: why did domain names cost $70? We assumed that it was just an arbitrary number that the powers that be had chosen; that's the way it had always been, so it never changed.

?!?!?!?!?!?!?!?

Rule: Don't be a baboon. Ever hear this analogy?

Week 1: Place six baboons in a room. On the ceiling fan, place a banana. Every time a baboon tries to reach for a banana, spray all the baboons with an ice-cold shower. It doesn't matter who reaches for the banana; all baboons get sprayed. After a week of research, no baboon in the room will attempt to reach for a banana.

Week 2: Take out one of the baboons and introduce a new one to the room. The first thing that the newcomer will do is reach for the banana on the ceiling fan. However, he will deal with great force and intimidation from the other baboons, since they, of course, know that his attempt will be followed by the ice-cold shower. After a while, the newcomer will stop attempting to reach for the banana, since anytime he does it, he's beaten up by five old-timers.

Week 3: Take yet another original baboon out of the pack, and introduce a new one. Observe the same scenario. Also, observe the newcomer from Week 2 admonishing the new baboon not to reach for the banana.

Week 4: Same thing. Now you've got three baboons from Week 1 and three new baboons.

Week 5: Same thing.

Week 6: Same thing.

Week 7: This is where it gets interesting. A brand new baboon is introduced, and none of the original baboons who were in Week 1 remain. However, observe how aggressively the newcomer will be "advised" when he tries to reach for the banana. Notice that none of the baboons currently in the room is aware of the ice-cold shower.

So why don't they reach for the banana?

Because that's the way they've always done it.

Don't be a baboon. Don't be afraid to break the rules and try it a new way.

So we're brainstorming. And again, that nagging concept of "$70–why?" keeps coming up. And we wonder, what exactly are you paying for? Technically, you're paying for virtual real estate. Your little space on the Internet. Your domain name.

But physically, you don't really *own* anything! And that's where our brainstorm took us.

Who in their right mind would pay $70 for something he doesn't even own? Something he can't physically touch?

Who would pay *anything* for it? Not that many people.

So why was it $70? Why wasn't it cheaper?

Why wasn't it . . . free?

And there you have reason 8,752 why brainstorming should be a part of your creative process, EVERY SINGLE TIME.

We came to the conclusion–why aren't domain names free? Why are we paying for what is basically a computer moving data around? We're not owning anything in the physical world– why is it so much money?

The answer, obviously, was that it shouldn't be. And that's what our client was trying to tell us. But, as we pointed out, it sounds a heck of a lot better the way we said it.

So . . . they came to us with the premise:

WE SELL DOMAIN NAMES CHEAPER.

We brainstormed, and came up with:

FIGHT THE POWER! DOMAIN NAMES SHOULD BE FREE–AND THURSDAY NIGHT, FOR ONE HOUR, THEY WILL BE!

We decided to pitch the client on this idea: give domain names away, for free, for one hour. Get your name out there– everyone would know about it. You'd take a financial hit, maybe $25k or so, but you should be able to make it up in volume the next day.

Viva la Revolution, indeed.

We figured we'd never get away with it. We assumed the pitch would fall flat just based on the "$25k hit" alone. We never thought it would get past the meeting room.

So we pitched. And they listened.

And then, much to the shock and dismay of me and my two employees who were sitting in the meeting with me, they said, "That sounds great! How do we do it?"

Thud, was the sound of our jaws hitting the floor.

?!?!?!?!?!?!?!?

> **Rule: Be prepared when the client occasionally surprises you and actually says YES.**

As I mentioned before, it's a rare event when you're dealing with "Can we *Do* that?!" type PR. Most clients, bosses, and the like, tend to take the safe road. So much, in fact, that you become accustomed to simply saying, "Ok, boss, I'll go rework that idea." It becomes safe. "Oh, Miller? He'll never approve it. I just go in for the meeting, then I have another three weeks to come back with something less daring."

Always be ready for that one day where Miller says, "Sure. Let's do it. Show me plans by Thursday."

We walked back to our office, with that sort of "now what?" look in our eyes. We now had to come up with a plan to give away domain names.

We had a million what-if's in our brain. What if no one took them? What if everyone took them, and no one came back? What if it put the client into bankruptcy, and they couldn't pay us?

?!?!?!?!?!?!?!?

> **Rule: If you constantly worry about the what-if's, you'll rarely get a chance to actually make the plan work. Stop worrying and build a plan. Then stick with it. Include in that plan how you're going to deal with any what-if's that come up, but don't waste time worrying about them.**

So we started. We had our idea: domain names should be free. We wanted to position this in such a way so we could make the client out to be the rebel of the industry. While the other domain name registrars were charging lots of money, we were going to be the upstart. The one who didn't. The one who came from behind and said, "There's a better way!" That was our job. We were going to make some noise by being smaller/better/faster.

Kind of like what my agency was doing.

The most pressing question was: How do you create need? How do you create what we would come to call "timely desire?" Timely desire, to us, meant getting people to want to do something in a specific amount of time.

We wanted people to come to one website during a certain amount of time. This meant creating timely desire to get them there.

The easiest way to create timely desire is to create a call to action. Simply let people know that if they don't do a certain thing, go to a certain place, whatever it might be, they're going to miss out.

Why do you think so many commercials end with "ONE WEEK ONLY!" or "The first 100 callers also get . . ." It's a call to action. An effective one, at that.

So we had our call to action. One hour. Come to this one website during this one specific time, and get one free domain name, totally free, for one year.

We knew that the client would take a financial hit, as we explained during the pitch. But we also knew it would be so much better than just sending out a release. We thought it was worth the cost, and surprisingly, our client did, too.

We had our call to action; we had our timely desire. Now we needed the press release to make it so.

The press release was a challenge. Not only did we have to impart a sense of urgency, but we also had to make it clear that our client wasn't a fly-by-night operation, and was really an accredited domain name registrar.

?!?!?!?!?!?!?!?

> **Rule:** When you're attempting to buck the system and cause a stir, make sure your credentials are still strong. You want to be able to say, "Yes, we're
>
> *(continued)*

rebels, but we're also this, this, and this." In other words, you can be the rebel doctor, but make sure you have your medical degree from the best med school in the country to prove it.

The release, after much tweaking, wound up looking like this:

RegisterFREE Offers Free Domain Registration For One Hour:

March 23rd, 2000, 9 P.M. Eastern Time RegisterFREE will provide Free Domain Name Registration, No Fee, No Strings.

Designed to Show That It Doesn't Have to Cost $70.00 to Register a Domain Name

New York (March 21, 2000): In an unprecedented effort to show the world that it shouldn't cost an arm and a leg to register a domain name of your own, RegisterFREE, the pioneers of low-cost domain name registration, today announced that for one hour, from 9 P.M. to 10 P.M. Eastern Time, on March 23rd, 2000, it will be free to register any available domain name for a full year.

"In offering free domain name registration for a full year, we are attempting to prove that it shouldn't cost $70.00, $50.00, or even $29.99 to register a domain name," said Antony Van Couvering, president of RegisterFree. "For a full hour on March 23, we're going to give away domain names in .com, .net, and .org for nothing. No strings attached, period, end of story."

"The fact is, you're not buying a physical item. You're not purchasing something that was built with materials and labor. You're buying a domain name, which is a database transaction, a piece of real estate on the Internet. This shouldn't be expensive. In fact, it should be free, and that's our ultimate goal," added Van Couvering.

"It's our hope that more companies in the domain registration field will drop their prices as well, since it's not costing these companies anywhere near what they're charging," Van Couvering noted.

RegisterFREE is currently the least expensive domain registrar in North America at $19.95. The Free Hour concept is simply to prove that it's not necessary to charge the exorbitant fees being charged today.

"We're already planning on doing another RegisterFree Free Hour in April, and another one in May. Again, our goal here is to make this process universally free," Van Couvering said.

And that was it. That was the release we came up with, and we hoped it would drive consumers to RegisterFree.com.

Little did we know how much it would.

We wrote the press release, and figured we should put it on the wire two days before the actual time of the event. This would give us a short window to pitch, but would allow us to target the specific editors we wanted, as well as the general public.

You know our feelings about wire services. They're a necessary evil, like spinach. You might not love them, but they serve a purpose on occasion. Remember, though, they're not catch-alls; you still have to do a lot of work, or your release won't matter.

When we issued the release on the wire, we did so mostly for the "Yahoo!" factor. That's when you issue a release and it immediately goes searchable on Yahoo!, Google, and other search engines. This is invaluable for those who might have news alerts set up–they get your information ASAP. But it also comes in handy based on how many people are reading the story at one time. The more who are reading (especially on Google), and the more who are writing about it themselves, the higher the story goes in relevance. This is described in greater detail in the Resources chapter at the end of this book.

So the release hit the wire. Most times when a release hits the wire, you wait to see it on your screen, then have some time to relax, put your notes together, get your media lists ready, and start doing follow-up within the hour.

PR Newswire called us to let us know that our release crossed at 9:52 A.M. on the 21st of March, 2000. "Thanks," we said. "Ok, guys," I said to my staff. "We should get started on pitching this story."

Some things you never forget. I was walking back to my desk (our office was a bullpen style–everyone saw everyone else at all times) when the main line rang. I remember the office assistant answering the phone and saying, "Yes, he's right here, hold on one second."

She punched the hold button, and looked directly at me. "Peter, CNN. Something about free domains."

The blood drained from my cheeks.

?!?!?!?!?!?!?!?

> **Rule:** Try not to let the blood drain from your cheeks. You'll look pretty weird.

"What do you mean they're on the phone? As in, calling us?"

My sarcastic assistant didn't miss a beat. "Yes, Peter. As in calling us. If they had sent a carrier pigeon, the phone wouldn't have rung."

I grabbed the phone nearest to where I was standing, while making a mental note to fire my assistant for the eighth time that day.

"Peter Shankman here."

"Hi, Peter. I'm a producer for CNN. We just noticed your press release about the free hour of domain names. Who can we talk to about this?"

That should have been my first warning. I called the client and said the line I love saying the most:

"I need you in 20 minutes to speak to CNN."

Those are the best lines to say, aren't they? Proves to the client you know what you're doing, thrills them that they're going to be on TV; it all works out. Those are the moments that make you remember why you got into PR in the first place.

We scheduled time and talking points for the interview, and just as we were about to hang up, I asked, "So, this is national. You do have enough bandwidth for this event, right? I mean, your servers can handle this, right?"

"Oh, sure," the client responded, without missing a beat. "Not a problem."

"Good," I said. "Wouldn't want to be on national TV and crash, huh?"

You're smart enough to see where this is going, right?

The next day and a half were spent coordinating interviews, both TV and print. *The Boston Globe*, CNN, even the Associated Press wanted to know not only what we were doing, but *why* we were doing it. That was the best part for me. The media's interest was piqued because of the why, which usually guarantees more press than simply the what.

?!?!?!?!?!?!?!?

> **Rule:** Get them interested in the WHY as much (if not more) than the what. The why will almost always make for a larger story.

The day of the event arrived, and we were all working overtime already. We went into lockdown mode. Lockdown is when employees know not to make any plans, that they'll be staying late. Food is on the company, along with anything else we might need to make us more productive.

?!?!?!?!?!?!?!?

> **Rule:** When asking more of your employees, make sure to provide more, as well. Be it as simple as pizza, or as complex as an on-site masseuse, reward them for going the extra mile.

We even had a fun moment, when a reporter doing a story interviewed the competitor to our client, the one who charged $70 per domain name. He kept asking why our client could be so cheap, and they so expensive, when it was, in effect, the same exact product.

The quote from the competitor went something like this:

"Some people just like driving BMWs, instead of a Yugo," she sniffed.

We made a spokesperson sniff. That was a highlight of our day.

The event was slated to run from 9 P.M. to 10 P.M., Eastern Time. We were ready to handle the onslaught of media response.

We were checking the domain name website every few minutes to make sure it was working, even though it wasn't our job. Our checker was reporting the site was up and running. A tiny bit slow, but nothing out of the ordinary. The three backup servers were functioning without a problem, as well.

Rule: If you can spare the manpower, have someone else double-check client information that you shouldn't have to do in the first place, just to be safe. Makes the client's job a lot easier, and keeps you up to speed on whatever might be going right or wrong.

The CNN story broke live on the Web at 4:15 P.M. EST. A great story, right on the front page of the site, telling the world that if they wanted a free domain name, they'd better hurry.

This was the fourth or fifth national exposure story of the day. *The Boston Globe* had run a piece earlier, both in print and online, and the *Los Angeles Times* had done something online that morning. Many, many smaller sites had made mention as well, and even Slashdot, the major tech geek portal website, had put up a story.

The CNN piece was the best, though. As I was picking up the phone to call the client no less than two minutes after the interview went live, I was interrupted by my assistant.

"Peter, their website is down."

For the second time in under 48 hours, the color drained from my cheeks.

"What do you mean, the website is down?"

"I can't get to it. I've tried refreshing, reloading, I can get to any other website, and my email works, it's not on my end."

I got on the phone and dialed the client, who answered in less than a ring.

"We know, we know. Server crashed. We're bringing it back online right now."

"What about the backup servers?" I asked.

"Yeah," he said. "We don't know why those didn't kick on immediately. We're looking into that."

Trying to stay as calm as humanly possible, I picked my words carefully.

"You told us the servers could handle the load of a national story. You mentioned you had numerous backup servers. You said this wouldn't be a problem. We've still got over four hours until the event actually takes place, and we're crashing NOW?"

?!?!?!?!?!?!?!?

> **Rule: Try really hard to never yell at a client. Nothing good ever comes from it.**

The client swore up and down that it was just a blip. They were working on it. I hung up, only quasi-reassured. To their credit, they were on it ASAP–they knew before we even called them that something was up.

A few minutes later, my assistant shouted out, "Hey, the site's back up again!"

"Whew," I said. "Ok. It was just a blip. That's good. Now, let's . . ."

"Oh, wait, it's down again."

"D'OH!"

What's that line? "Welcome to my nightmare, come on in, the water's fine." That was us. The site would go up, a thousand people would try to sign up, the site would go down.

Fortunately, our client was not only smart, but well connected. In under an hour, he'd lined up three different companies who had servers they could borrow, and they were finishing setting them up, load-balancing them, and making sure all was right.

It was. The servers worked flawlessly for the next few hours, and everything seemed Ok. The site was noticeably slower, but it was working. People could still buy domain names.

Would it last? What do you think?

8 P.M. comes. Pizza arrives. We're chowing down, sitting around multiple monitors, watching the news . . . waiting. The hardest part.

Roles we assigned:

One employee to watch the site

One employee to watch the news/wires/alerts

One employee to monitor chat rooms

An open conference call (phone, basically) that had an open line with not only the client, but the other sites where the computers were. This was hugely valuable.

> **Rule:** When doing a big event, always have an open line, even if you never use it. Just reserve a conference line (see the Resources chapter) and keep it open. Worst case, you can shout out, and the client will hear you, no matter where you both are geographically. It's worth it.

Finally, we had an intern just roaming. At the computer, on call to get us sodas, basically, doing whatever we needed so we didn't have to leave our chairs.

> **Rule:** If you can spare the manpower, during events that require constant and immediate attention, have someone be a roamer. You can just shout out his or her name and get whatever you need. You'll find it very handy for things like coffee, bathroom breaks ("Sit here and watch this screen. I'll be right back."), and other items for which you'd normally leave your desk.

So here's the way the timeline broke down:

8:50 P.M.: Site was still up. Charts were telling us that people were signing on and reloading to see if the event had started. Site, however, was still live.

8:52 P.M.: The chat rooms and websites are going off the wall, people talking about what domains they wanted, how many they thought they could get, if it would even work at all, etc. . . .

8:55 P.M.: We took one last deep breath, sure we wouldn't get another one until this thing was over.

9:00 P.M.: The free domain name page went live.

9:00 P.M. and 32 seconds: The site crashed.

9:02 P.M.: It was brought back up, and the first people started registering their domain names.

9:10 P.M.: We'd gotten over 200 domain names registered in the first three or four minutes. Before the site crashed again. And was brought back up again. And crashed again.

Welcome to our hour. This was basically it. A few hundred people would register names, then the site would crash. They'd reboot; the site would crash again. They'd reboot again, and so on, and so on.

While lots of people were able to get to the site and register, lots more couldn't. And those were the people who made the most noise, naturally.

In the end, the site registered, in that hour, approximately 12,000 domain names. Not bad for a website that kept going down, on average, once every two minutes. (Load balancing, my foot!)

We tried to keep calm, keep breathing. . . . Of course, the first press calls started coming in almost immediately after the site crashed for the first time. We'd expected that, so we kept the basic party line much like we'd said all night:

We are aware that some people are having a hard time getting to RegisterFree.com. At this time, an unprecedented amount of people are responding to this event, and of course, no site would be able to handle this amount of traffic. So, we're making sure the bandwidth we have is being properly allocated to serve the maximum number of registrants possible tonight. We'll have more to say immediately following our free hour.

Once the promotion ended, we put up a placeholder site, letting people know that there'd be another promotion similar to this very soon, and thanking everyone who registered and tried to register.

We also issued a press release, immediately informing people of what was going on:

Ladies and Gentlemen:

This was truly awesome. We never expected ANYTHING like the AMAZING response we received to our RegisterFREE Free Hour Promotion. At certain times over the course of the evening, the NSI registry (the universal database that provides domain name availability checks) was unable to process requests for those domain name availability checks. As a result, traffic was significantly slowed at times, and some people were unable to register their domain name. We hope to receive better support from the NSI Registry during our next promotion, which will be coming up very shortly. We can safely say that hundreds of thousands of people came to RegisterFREE.com tonight, and thousands were able to register their domain name for free. At this point, we ask all those who were unable to register a domain name to send an email to cs@registerfree.com and let us know, so we can deal with each query personally. Congratulations to all of those customers who did get through and were able to submit their registration request. RegisterFREE.com STRONGLY believes that Domain Name Registration should be 100 percent free, and we will have this promotion again very soon. Again, thank you for your continued patience and support as we try to make all domain names 100 percent free.

–The RegisterFREE team

And there you have it.

?!?!?!?!?!?!?!?

> **Rule:** Know how to react to the situation. Always have the press release ready to go, not only to the media, but up online somewhere so that people understand where you're coming from. Remember—it's your (and your client's) reputation on the line. Especially for high-profile events, you want to make sure that you have all the answers for whatever questions can be thrown at you, as well as whatever happens to come, unpredictably, out of left field.

In this case, our left field was the overwhelming response we got from the promotion. We knew we'd get a reaction, but had no idea where it would go. Would it be huge? Would it be massive? How were we to know? We hoped it would, but could never have imagined it would be as big as it got.

Your job, as stunt-creators, as PR people, as magicians, is to make sure you (and your clients or staff) are aware of what you're doing—and what repercussions can come from what you're doing.

Doing a promotion in a parking lot with a celebrity? What about a stampede? Do you have a way to get the celebrity out of there if things get hairy? What about crowd control? What if it's 110 degrees? Do you have hoses to cool everyone down? What if there's a monsoon? Seriously—these are the things for which we have to plan, regardless of how doubtful it is that (1) they'll ever happen, or (2) the client will even approve the stunt in the first place.

Imagine the plan being plagued with the most far-fetched, implausible things that could ever, ever happen. Then take it a step further before you implement it. The fact is, we didn't think hundreds of thousands of people would show up to try and get a free domain name. But they did.

?!?!?!?!?!?!?!?

> **Rule:** When a client says, "Oh, yeah, of course we've got the bandwidth," confirm it. This goes for whatever the client says. "Sure, we've got the rights to use that music." Confirm it. "No, the celebrity loves us—she'll be there." Confirm it.

Confirm it, confirm it, confirm it.

We had hundreds of thousands of people try to access a site that was built to hold maybe 10,000 or 20,000. Doesn't cut it. People couldn't get in; they weren't happy.

> **Rule:** It's always an easier job to do pre-cleanup then post-cleanup. It's like throwing a party where you can have one of two jobs: cleaning the place before the party, where you have to dust, vacuum, and fluff the couch pillows; or cleaning the place after the party, where you have to dump the full ashtrays, clean the half-drank, lipstick-smeared glasses, and mop up the spilled artichoke dip. Which one sounds easier? Choose option #3: if you assign people to clean up over the course of the party, you'll have less to do when it's finally over.

In the end, though, a promotion should do one thing–promote. We were hired to promote RegisterFree.com to the world. To let people who wanted to register domain names know that it didn't need to cost an arm and a leg to do it. It could be cheap, it could be easy, and it shouldn't be controlled by one entity. That was our job, that's what we were paid to do. We were hired to do it in such a way that it got to the most people in the shortest amount of time possible, and in the most efficient way.

Did we do that? Well, consider this: the day after the RegisterFree.com promotion, RegisterFree.com registered over 1,000 domain names at $19.95. The following day, over 2,000 domain names at $19.95.

RegisterFree.com has since been sold, and I'm sure the founder is onto his next great idea. But here's the kicker: If you've registered a domain name anywhere lately, you've noticed the cost . . . $8.99? $5.99? Free?

I'd say we did our job. It cost us a few headaches, some quickly written explanations of what happened and when, but in the end, we did what we were hired to do. We did it well, we got a message out, we got the *right* message out, in a 99.9 percent positive light. The client was happy, consumers were happy, and the media was happy.

And eventually, we even got to go home and get some sleep.

WHAT WE LEARNED
FROM THIS CHAPTER

1. At some point, a client is going to say yes to an idea—even a totally off-the-wall one. Be ready to deal with that.

2. Don't be a baboon. Be ready to try something new, a different way. Just because you're accustomed to doing things a certain way doesn't mean it's the absolute right way—especially not in every situation. Times change, things evolve. If you don't, or if you refuse to, you'll eventually be eliminated. (That goes for life, as well as PR!)

3. On the day of a specific stunt, have everything planned and ready: know which employees are going to do which jobs, and make sure they're adequately equipped to do their jobs.

4. Pay for the pizza: Your employees, consultants, and staff will be working their butts off on the day of the event. Take care of them. Have their favorite food, drinks, energy bars, whatever, ready for them, and have lots of it. Also, think about something for them for afterwards—a spa day, a round of golf, Mets tickets, whatever they like. Everybody likes to be appreciated.

5. Have it ready—the release, the counter-release, the back up statement, the "It went well!" statement, the "It went just Ok" statement, and the "We never expected 84 million people to overrun the government" statement. Be prepared.

6. Finally, check, check, and triple-check. Client says they're prepped. Confirm that they are. Client says they have the bandwidth. Make sure they do.

7. It's these types of events, when done well, that get you into the history books. Never forget your chance for greatness can come from these stunts, in addition to making the client or boss happy. Always be looking ahead—what's next? What will this do? How will this skyrocket us, our profiles, our budgets, for the next "great thing?"

CHAPTER 8

What Happens When You Lose Your Voice?

HOW DO YOU DO PR WHEN YOU'RE NOT ALLOWED TO TALK?

So let me set the scene for you.

It's a random Friday morning. You're just getting into the office, perhaps a little later than usual, after a really crazy Thursday night out with the guys (or girls). You get to the office, thrilled that it's Friday. It should be an easy day. You're hoping so, anyway. After all, that headache you have won't go away by itself.

You get to your desk, sit down with your Venti Skim Latte, secure that by the time you finish your coffee, the aspirin you took for your hangover will be doing the job.

"Whew. It's Friday," you think. Easy day.

Then the phone rings. Expecting it to be a buddy, recounting the escapades of the previous night, you answer the phone.

"Hi, this is so-and-so with the *New York Times*. We're planning on breaking a story tomorrow morning about a federal investigation into the methods used by <insert any client who you're working with here>, and we're wondering what comment they might have."

All of a sudden, those two aspirin aren't going to be anywhere near enough.

Or, let's look at it another way. . . .

You're fast asleep, having nodded off somewhere between the 11 P.M. news and Letterman. The phone rings, you glance at the digital clock by your bed, as you groggily pick it up: 2:30 A.M.

"Hello," you mutter.

"Hi, this is <assistant to major client CEO>. He was just arrested and charged with attempting to pick up a minor that he met on the Internet for sexual purposes. The *LA Times* was there at the police station, and got wind of the story. They want to run with it. What do we do?"

Ah, crises. They're just so darn inconvenient, aren't they?

What follows is sort of a primer. No two crises are the same, and no crisis will fit perfectly into any given mold. What I've put together here are the basics. What to do, how to do it, and general ideas on what to do with the staff, employees, media, and the like. Tailor it to your needs. Change it, or even ignore parts of it if they don't apply to you. Just remember the number one rule: A crisis doesn't respect anything. Not the 9-to-5, not the weekend off, not the holiday, or the kid's birthday, or the company picnic, or the CEO who's in the air and can't be reached.

?!?!?!?!?!?!?!?

Rule: Crises, by nature, are pretty darn disrespectful.

WHAT YOU SHOULD BE DOING WHEN THERE ISN'T A CRISIS CURRENTLY ENGULFING YOUR WORLD

Let's talk for a second about the Federal Emergency Management Agency (FEMA). Apart from their disastrous handling of the press that resulted from their management of Hurricane Katrina, they do one thing very well: they go around teaching preparedness. They might not know how to talk to Anderson Cooper to save their lives, but they know how to prepare you for a hurricane, or tornado, or terrorist attack. They know disaster prep.

FEMA are the folks who teach you how to keep a "go bag" next to your front door so you can get out in a hurry if you have to. They teach you what to keep in it. What to carry on you at all times.

So, stealing a page from their playbook, has anyone taught you preparedness?

What's the first thing that you'd do if a client called with a crisis? Do you have a plan in place? Are you prepared? You are? Great. What if you're on vacation when the call comes in? Or in a plane? Or scuba diving? Or pitching the largest pitch of your life? Or talking live to MSNBC?

Then what?

Your first job, prior to any crisis, is to make sure that you're equipped to handle it. You wouldn't fight a fire without the right equipment, so why would you try to handle a crisis without being prepared? You wouldn't.

Create a checklist. This checklist should have everything you need to do in case of a crisis, from the moment you become aware of it, until it's over or out of your hands entirely.

At The Geek Factory, our initial checklist has the following rules.

?!?!?!?!?!?!?!?

> **Rule: Thou shall have a call log.**

Your call log is your first line of information. It tells how you got the information in the first place. (Excellent in case the lawyers get involved.) It contains the basic facts: how the information came in (call, email, fax, website, etc.), who got it to you, contact info, if you have it. If it came from a website, do you have an IP trace? If it came in via fax, do you have a return number? Email—was it a real email? The basic facts. Having those allows you to start your paper trail immediately.

Get as much information as humanly possible, but don't get all "in their face" about it. Get as many facts as you possibly can, but don't waste time trying to coax information out of people who don't want to give it. You can get the rest later. If nothing else, get the wording of the exact problem. (Example: The *Los Angeles Times* will be *printing* in *tomorrow's edition* that they have proof that the *company has been secretly dumping toxic waste into the Pacific for 15 years.*)

That's the information you need. At this point, asking where they got their information is not your job, nor the most critical factor for you to deal with. You need to get the people that matter together and deal with the problem. To do that, you need to get in touch with them. How?

?!?!?!?!?!?!?!?!

> ## Rule: Thou shall have an updated contact list.

Do you know how to get in touch with your CEO? How about the CFO? Do you know your company's (or client's) law firm's phone number? (For that matter, do you even know the name of the law firm?) How about the mobile phone number of the person at the law firm assigned to your company or client?

Put together an all-encompassing contact list—not only of key employees, but key consultants (lawyers, accountants) key customers who will go on record in your favor, and even, if you're big enough and have friends in high places, politicians or celebrities who will talk in your favor.

You'll want to keep this list protected, and only give it to those who matter. A list with phone numbers, contact information, and the like, of top-level people in your company or client's company, should not be taken lightly. Give it out sparingly, but make sure there's access to it when needed. It's a fine line to walk.

So you have the contact list. But how do you know who to call?

At the Factory, we work with the word PoLiCE. As in, police the situation. Take control. The P means call the Public Relations head (this could be the Director of Marketing, the PR VP, whomever is designated as either the spokesperson or the leader of crisis management). Follow that up immediately with L for Legal. Let your legal department know to go on standby–they're going to be getting a call rather soon from the CEO or whomever is designated. The C stands for CEO, or whomever is in charge. Finally, everyone else. We'll get to them in a second.

PR, Legal, CEO. Those are your three main people to contact. They need to know what's going on, what the latest situation is, and what's going to happen next. You'll keep them informed until such time as they're in control. Your job is to keep the plane steady until you, the CEO, and legal can sit down and map out a new course. Basically, you want to make sure those who matter know what's going on until you can all sit down and formulate a plan.

Let's discuss for a second the *E* in PoLiCE. The *E* stands for everyone. In order to better understand who "everyone" is, we have to discuss rumors.

My first job after I graduated from college was in a major media company. I was a grunt, working in their newsroom, virtually 24 hours a day. I loved it, though. It was such a rush. Then I walked in one morning, and several people came up to me: "I heard we're losing our jobs." "I heard there are massive layoffs coming today . . ." "I heard people were being escorted out . . ." Blah, blah, blah.

Basically, by the time the layoffs came, later in the day, everyone already knew. The media knew. Families knew. It was handled not in the best of ways. It could have been done a lot better.

All because someone told someone else, and the rumors flew.

As we all know, that's what happens when someone's got loose lips–everyone knows everything in about two seconds.

Because of that, we need to know about the *E* and understand what it means. See, if everyone knows, it's not necessarily a bad thing. In fact, everyone of your employees or staff *should* know! But it should be done on your terms.

Rumors cause people to communicate poorly. Miscommunication is your enemy. One of your many, many jobs is to control rumors. The goal is to prevent the rumors from getting out. But how?

Control the flow of information. When we have a crisis situation start to unfold with one of our clients, we immediately advise them to send out a note to all employees, alerting them that any employee who talks to the media without authorization can be terminated for cause.

This usually keeps the rumors, and more importantly, people speaking out of turn, to a minimum.

So your first job is completed. You've gotten control of the initial situation, and told people who need to be told, and told those who don't need to know to shut the heck up.

Ok. Now what?

?!?!?!?!?!?!?!?

> **Rule: No matter how many people, there is only one voice.**
>
> The key to surviving any crisis, bar none, is to have one statement. For every five employees, there are ten versions as to what happened. So the key is to only have one statement. Only one person can talk, only one voice shall be heard.
>
> And that shall be the law.

The phrase too many cooks comes to mind. Well, too many spokespeople, same thing.

Thus, you must implement the Commandment of Crisis Management: Only one person shall speak for the company. One face of the company, one statement, one voice. You shall become a collective, with one person speaking for the collective. That one person might have been molded by 50 different executives, each offering advice, but in the end, one person talks to the media, to the public, to the shareholders, and to the employees.

So one person talks to the media, and everyone else has been threatened with death if they say anything. Now what?

Well, you've given your initial statement to the media. It sounded something like this:

> Today, Acme Corporation was informed by the Department of Justice that an investigation is underway regarding alleged accounting improprieties involving Acme Corporation's finances for calendar years ending 2002, 2003, and 2004. Acme Corporation is cooperating fully with the Justice Department. At this point, due to the status of the investigation, we have no further comment.

Now is not the time to defend your client's innocence. It's not the time to engage in debate. There'll be time for that later. Now your job is to inform the media when your client has something to say, and keep your mouth shut when it doesn't. It's that simple.

Rule: Thou shalt create an all hands update.

You're going to want to let everyone know exactly what's going on, but you're going to want to do it in a way that secures your client's privacy as much as possible. Assume anything you say to your employees will somehow wind up on Gawker.com, Drudge Report, or worse.

Instruct your client to draft an internal email and read it to their employees. (Usually, that means drafting one for the client, and giving it to them.) If at all possible, the client should read it, and not mail it out. If you have an organization all in one office building, call them all in for a conference or meeting. If the client sends out an email to the entire company, it *will* get to the media. Don't ask how, and don't waste time trying to understand where the leak came from. Just accept that it will happen, and don't send out anything that you wouldn't want to see in print. If your client has numerous offices or sites, try to arrange a conference or video call, either via phone or satellite feed. You're doing this to keep the client morale up, to explain exactly what happened, and to remind your client, yet once again, that they should not be speaking to any media. You can't reinforce this enough. In the end, the client will be the one speaking to his employees, but there's no reason he can't speak your words. It's your job to keep him calm, anyway.

?!?!?!?!?!?!?!?!?

Rule: Thou shalt use technology to thy advantage.

Stop into the chat rooms and message boards and read. What is the public saying about your client's company? If they're publicly traded, what are the market websites (Yahoo!, Motley Fool, etc.) saying about them in their chat rooms and message boards? How can you use this information to craft a well-worded response to the media? Note: Do not, under any circumstances, respond to any messages or chat requests and don't let the client, either, no matter how tempting it might be to do so. Online bulletin boards and chat rooms are not the place to preach your client's philosophy or try to prove their innocence. Just read what other people are saying, and try to gauge reaction.

See where are we going here? The key here is not only to work the crisis, but to stay informed. If it's a typical crisis, people will be concerned, upset, confused, and yes, even fearful—of their jobs, of the public, you name it. There's a reason the word "crisis" isn't all cute and cuddly. If a crisis was cute and cuddly, it'd be named something more fitting, like, "puppy."

MORE THINGS TO DO THAT SHOULD GO WITHOUT SAYING BUT ARE INEVITABLY FORGOTTEN

Stay in contact: make sure your voice mail message has alternate ways for the media to reach you. You need to be 100 percent, completely accessible to the press for as long as the crisis lasts. If this means canceling personal plans, so be it, or at least be reachable and ready to respond at a moment's notice. All media employees at The Geek Factory have alternate phone, email, pager, and cellular information on their outgoing voice mail. In addition, all employees have access to the Internet from home, allowing them to keep in touch with the office at any time, day or night, weekday or weekend.

Rule: Thou shall keep the head honchos informed.

Make sure the client keeps its upper management updated. Over the course of the day, have the client send out a few brief emails, offering updates as to what's going on, and what's expected to happen. By keeping upper management updated, you're allowing for a better flow of communication throughout the company.

Rule: Thou shalt track and clip.

If you don't already use one, consider hiring both an online and offline clipping service to follow what's being said about your client company. Luce and Burrell's are two such services, but there are many more out there. These companies will track all forms of media coverage, both online and traditional, about your company and the selected keywords you give them.

Change the term "client" to "you" in the paragraphs above, and these rules will work just as well when it's your company in a crisis.

One of the easiest ways to get into trouble during a crisis is to forget who you're talking to. It's a crisis. You're more than likely handling the majority of it yourself, and the client is looking to you for guidance, support, and a general "what do we do next, please tell us it'll be OK" vibe.

That can get a little tough on you, especially if you don't have a huge support staff with whom you can work through it.

What you have to remember though (and tattoo it on the insides of your eyelids, if need be), is that while you can be friends with the media, they're most likely not your confidants, and if you talk to them "off the record," there's a good chance your words will come back to bite you.

This is not a slam or dig at the media in any way. The majority of media are good, decent people. I'm friends with many of them! But they have a job to do. And if you're talking to them over a beer, and you mention how depressed you are because you're just sure your boss is guilty, well, you've gone and put the reporter in a horrible spot.

You don't want to do that. Tell a therapist. Not a reporter.

Remember how mom always taught us to tell the truth?

?!?!?!?!?!?!?!?

> **Rule: Yet again, mom was right about something: Don't lie.**

Don't lie. If you don't know the answer, don't answer the question. An "I'll get back to you on that" is ALWAYS a better answer than a made up one. The fact remains, if you lie about something and you're quoted on it in the media, it's going to be with you for the rest of your company's life until you're caught. And usually, you'll be caught a lot quicker than you imagine.

Simply say, "That's a good question. I'm going to check on it and get back to you in 20 minutes." Then do it. Don't leave the reporter without a call back. Even if you call back to let the reporter know that you're still looking for the information, that's better than leaving them hanging.

True story: had a friend who was on point to the media. Reporter called him and asked him a question. Friend didn't know the answer and said, "I'll get back to you within 20 minutes."

CEO called my friend into a meeting. My friend forgot about the reporter. Story the next day: "Company XYZ had no comment about the allegations."

CEO's first words to my friend: "Tell us exactly why we hired you, if we have no comment?"

Ask yourself. Is that the conversation you really want to be having with your CEO? Ever?

Let's talk for a second about emotions.

Emotions are great in your personal life. They dictate what to do in several circumstances (i.e., when to propose marriage, when to say, "I love you," and when to snuggle a seven-week-old kitten). Emotions are great. We have them for a reason.

Ninety-nine percent of the time, however, they have absolutely no place whatsoever in business. This goes triple for public relations.

It's not personal. Above all else, you've got to remember that if you want to be thought of as someone who can be counted on in a crisis.

Scenario:

You've been working with a reporter on a story for weeks. You've gotten him interviews, unprecedented access to the company, and exclusive quotes. You've set up photo opportunities, rearranged executives' schedules to be in town at the right time, and have annoyed enough people in your company to get this article done.

The day comes. You get in early, go online to read it. And . . .

There's a total of one mention of your client, calling them "another player in the space." No photos. No artwork. No quotes.

You sit there, stunned, wondering what alternate universe you just stepped into.

You've just entered what I call the "five stages of PR grieving." Similar to the "five stages of grieving," the five stages of PR grieving will affect us all, more than once. If you've never been affected by the five stages of PR grieving and you've been working in PR for over five years, give me a call, I'd like to hire you.

Stage 1: Denial

There's no way they left us out. My newspaper is probably just missing a page. After all I did for that reporter? No way. We're in there. I'm looking at the wrong section. It's obviously here; the story obviously ran; I'll just reread the entire newspaper until I find it.

Stage 2: Anger

That stupid reporter. Does he have any idea how much I moved the world to get him all the information he needed? I dragged the CEO back from Geneva for this meeting! And what did it get me? Nothing! I'm never speaking to him again. He thinks he covers this beat? I COVER THIS BEAT. I'll beat him! He's never going to get another quote from my company again!

Stage 3: Bargaining

Ok, I don't hate that reporter. I'm going to call him up and be very nice and totally suck up to him and convince him to write another story. I know he rules the news, and I just have to deal with it and be nice and get a new story. I can do it. Easy.

Stage 4: Depression

They're never going to cover us again. Forget it. I'm going to take out my resume and polish it up. Oh, who am I kidding, I'll never get another job in this industry again. I'm going to learn how to install custom rims on cars. That's what I'll do. A fresh start.

And finally, Stage 5: Acceptance

Ok. So they didn't include us. It happens. We'll get through it. In the meantime, let me write up a quick email to the boss explaining what happened, why it happened, and what I'm going to do to prevent it in the future.

And there you have it. The five stages of PR grieving.

It happens to all of us, sooner or later, and it's going to happen more than once. We can't prevent it–the best thing we can do is adapt to it so it doesn't permanently affect us, and we don't do anything we'll regret.

?!?!?!?!?!?!?!?

> **Rule: Old skydiving (or any extreme sport) adage: You'll be fine, as long as you don't do anything stupid.**

You've just been gut-kicked in the form of a story that didn't include you. Your first reaction is a nasty email to the reporter, chastising him, cc'ing his editor, asking how he could be so stupid as to ignore your client or company. Didn't he do any research at all? Where did he get his degree, Wal-Mart?

I don't actually have to tell you not to do that, right?

In my office, whenever a story comes out that doesn't include our client, whether it was an oversight or edit by the reporter, or just a mistake on the part of my employee, I make the employee take a 20-minute walk before responding to either the reporter or the client.

It's a smart move–it lets the blood come down to simmer from boil, lets the employee figure out how he really wants to deal with it. Does he want to email the reporter first? If so, what's he going to say? Does he want to call the client first before the client calls him? If so, what's he going to say?

Never underestimate the power of a walk in situations like this. It lets you breathe and plot your next move. It lets you reevaluate. The military strategist Sun Tzu was a huge fan of getting out of the office and reevaluating. Of course, in his day, you got off the battlefield and re-strategized your entire army, but you get the idea.

Once back from your walk, deep breaths taken, you can sit down and figure out how to approach your reporter. You know best–is it email, a phone call, carrier pigeon? What works best in your relationship? If it's an email, stick to the facts. Don't be accusatory, don't blame. You're just calmly emailing to try and find out what happened. So it's something like this, perhaps:

?!

Dear John:

Just wanted to drop you a note. I read your piece this morning on the salmon industry—well done, it's a really detailed piece. I was kind of surprised, though, to find that company X only had a one line description, especially after all the time you and I spent coordinating, getting the photo shoots ready, etc. I do hope you didn't run into any problems, and I want to make sure that my staff was as helpful as they could possibly be to you. In other words, I want to make sure it wasn't something we did (or didn't do) on this end.

Just let me know when you have a second. Thanks. Again, good piece. Well done.

All the best,

—Peter

?!

Basic, to the point. Nonaccusatory, calm in tone. "More flies with honey than vinegar" has never been so relevant.

Back to our crisis.

If you've been working with reporters the way I've been suggesting, then you've made a few friends. A few reporters who, even though they might cover you in a light that isn't necessarily the most flattering, will be straight with you, and give you what they know.

Contrary to popular belief, it's not a reporter's job to screw you. A reporter doesn't wake up in the morning and say, "Hey, let's see how I can mess with Peter's company today."

But, it is a reporter's job to report the news. And when your CEO has been busted, when your industry is up 22 percent this quarter yet your company is down 16 percent, when there's been a shooting in your cafeteria, or your drug has just been blamed for the temporary blindness of 300 people in the Midwest, you're news, and you are to be reported on.

?!?!?!?!?!?!?!?

Rule: Don't hate the player. Hate the game.

Reporters and publicists live in a symbiotic balance. We try and help them, thus they can help us. When this balance is upset, by say, an editor who cuts the entire section pertaining to your company out of the story, it's our job to rebalance the equation. The best way to do that, as mentioned previously, is honesty.

The reporter knows you'll be upset. He knows that you'll be getting pounded from several different directions—the CEO, the shareholders, the client as a whole. Anyone and everyone looking for someone to blame will come down on the PR person—if it's a crisis, "How could you let them print that?" If it's a story without you, "How could you let them miss us?"

Either way, it's going to be your fault. The media knows this. Like I said, I've yet to see a reporter deliberately bash a client of mine just because he wanted to make it personal. Reporters don't do that. Not only is it bad karma, but it totally undermines their credibility. If a reporter bashes a client, there's a reason for it. And sometimes, all the good PR in the world can't prevent it.

If a client is kept out of a story despite your best efforts, one of two things has probably happened. Either the reporter didn't find the story viable enough (in which case, you need to go back and refine your pitch or find new news) or the editor killed it for space, or other reasons. Either way, your email to the reporter should ask why.

?!?!?!?!?!?!?!?

Rule: Learn from being cut from a story.

Finally, keep in mind that today's major crisis is tomorrow's old news. It's very rare that a company in the harsh media spotlight of crisis stays there for long. In the end, you're a spoke on the wheel. That wheel might be turning a bit slowly, but it's turning. And the media wheel will soon turn to the next company, and you'll be off the hook. You might have a little cleanup to do, but you'll emerge from this crisis smarter, stronger, and a bit leaner—ready to face down the next crisis.

In the end, you'll soon have that carefree Friday morning back. But perhaps this time, instead of nursing your headache, you'll use the downtime to update your emergency contact list.

WHAT WE LEARNED
FROM THIS CHAPTER

1. Crises will happen. Nothing you can do or say will prevent them. Eventually, they'll happen. It's what you do or say during and after the crisis that will define you.

2. Don't be a part of the problem. Have a road map laid out way before a crisis ever rears its ugly head. Be prepared. Preparedness goes a long way in fighting the fire.

3. Keep the top brass updated at all times. Make sure those who should be in the loop are in the loop. Make sure those who don't need to be aren't, and are kept silent.

4. Be reachable.

5. Hate the game, not the player. Don't fight with the journalist. He or she is doing a job.

6. It's never personal.

?!

CHAPTER 9

You Don't Have to Run Over Someone to Get Press

HOW THE SIMPLE ACT OF TURNING 30 PRODUCED THE GREATEST BIRTHDAY PARTY OF THE YEAR

Ever hear that old joke about the military cadet at the ball? He goes up to a woman, grabs her, and says, "Hey baby! Let's get out on the dance floor and make some magic!"

The woman, very prim and proper, says "Unhand me, you savage beast! Don't you know who I am? I am the wife of the General of this base!"

The cadet stops, looks at the General's wife. Stands up to his full height, and says, "Well, lady, don't you know who *I* am?"

"I do not," she replies.

"Good," says the cadet, as he fades into the crowd.

Moral of the story? Just because you're not a nationally recognized face, doesn't mean you can't act like you are. In fact, sometimes it even helps if you're not!

The scene: Late spring, 2002. I was 29 years old, still on a high from selling my first PR firm a year before. Working as a consultant to a bunch of different clients, I was traveling all over the world for them, spending almost all of my time on a plane, in general, just having a great time–definitely above average for the normal 29-year-old.

I was quickly approaching my thirtieth birthday, and experiencing the typical "Oh, man, I'm gonna be 30 . . . I can't believe this. . . . I feel so *old*!" issues that everyone has.

I'd known for quite some time that I'd wanted to throw a party. I figured I'd take over a bar somewhere, invite some friends, it would be fun. But something was nagging at me . . . something I couldn't quite put my finger on.

See, if you've read this much, you know that doing things the ordinary way is a sure path to boredom and complacency. I've never done things like that. By coming up with new and random ideas, you continually challenge the mind, push the boundaries, and achieve greatness. It's simply how it works.

So for me, to just "invite some friends to a bar and drink," didn't lend itself well to my way of thinking. Something about it just didn't feel like me. No matter which bar or club I checked out, I just wasn't feeling it. My gut was telling me that a gathering of friends in a bar just wasn't what I was supposed to be doing. (I didn't know why, but my gut was talking. When it does, I tend to listen to it.)

?!?!?!?!?!?!?!?

> **Rule:** We have gut instincts for a reason. We need to pay attention to them in order to survive at optimum performance. We tend to get into trouble when we don't listen to our gut instincts. They're a basic part of who we are, and they're designed to protect us. If something doesn't feel right, either professionally or personally, figure out why, and fix it. There's a reason for that feeling.

In the end, I just knew that I could do more—that turning 30 was a milestone—something worthy of being treated the way you'd treat any milestone. And of course, because it was me, it had to be done bigger, stronger, louder, and faster.

You know, in typical "Can we *do* that?" style.

As always, I started with a brainstorm. What would make the perfect thirtieth birthday? Well, it had to be big. I wanted all my friends to be there, and because I had a lot of friends who lived outside New York, it had to be worthy of their time to attend. (Not that I'm not worthy on my own, mind you, but for a friend of mine to hop a flight from London or Minsk to come to New York and hang out with me for the night, well, it better be more than just me standing there holding a drink.)

It would also have to be fun. If it was going to be big, it was going to take some planning and a lot of time. I didn't want to work on a project that would bore me or not get me excited.

?!?!?!?!?!?!?!?

> **Rule:** When choosing a client, try to figure out how to work with clients that are fun and exciting. Sometimes we have to take on clients without much of a choice because, hey, they're paying the bills. But even then, try and figure out what's exciting about them. Find out from different sources within the client—there's a reason people work there—there must be something exciting about the place. Work that angle, all the time. Never forget about it. It's what turns mundane into exciting, and what turns an ordinary pitch into a brilliant story.

Ok. So it had to be a major party, an event, as it were. It had to be exciting. And since it was coming up on early June and my birthday was in August, it had to be something that didn't require six months of planning.

Despite my wanting it to be big and exciting, the goal was really, first and foremost, to keep it simple. Finding the proper balance between excitement, brilliance, and simplicity is an art form. Once you get it, you become known as a miracle worker, i.e., "I can't believe he pulled this huge and complex event off! He doesn't even look like he worked up a sweat!"

?!?!?!?!?!?!?!?

> **Rule:** Exciting and brilliant doesn't mean difficult. If you're organized, efficient, and most importantly, *creative,* you can pull off anything, regardless of how brilliant and exciting it is.

Well, what's simple? A party is simple. Hire a caterer, reserve a space, reserve a band, get alcohol, hire servers. If I could somehow make it "a party to remember," then it would be worth it.

?!?!?!?!?!?!?!?

> **Rule:** Whatever plan you make for an event or stunt, try to take it one level above what you think you'll get. That then gives you something to shoot for.

What could I do to take my event to the next level?

I thought about hiring people, perhaps entertainers, or maybe a musical act. But they would be expensive! I wasn't a giant company with an unlimited budget. I was a guy turning 30. And although I might have been a little more well-known than your average guy, it wasn't like companies were calling me up asking for my permission to give me free stuff.

And then, much to my satisfaction, I had one of my wonderful "Ah-HA!" moments.

I simply asked myself, "Why weren't they?"

Why weren't companies pounding down my door to try to give me free stuff? I know a ton of people. I'm intelligent. I'm moderately handsome. I talk to everyone. I have good posture.

Why weren't they, indeed!

?!?!?!?!?!?!?!?

> **Rule:** It's the simplest, easiest questions that wind up doing you the most good. Ask them. To yourself, to friends, to clients, to your dog. Ask them. Often.

So there I was. Sitting at my computer, making a list of companies that I wanted to sponsor my thirtieth birthday party. I remember having dinner with a friend that night, and telling her my plan.

"You're insane," was her only response. She apologized after the party.

So what kind of companies would (1) I want to sponsor my party, and (2) I want to sponsor my party?

Well, what kind of companies do I like? And what kind of companies do my friends like? And most importantly, who do I know who works for those companies? Finally, what kind of companies would benefit from sponsoring my birthday party?

?!?!?!?!?!?!?

> **Rule:** Low-hanging fruit, while not necessarily always the sweetest, certainly goes a long way toward fulfilling your initial hunger.

Who did I know? Well, I knew a lot of people. I knew people at Sony. I knew people at Sebastian Hair Care. I knew people at Downtime Day Spa. I knew people at Viacom, Yoo-hoo Chocolate Drink, New Frontier Media, Sin City Entertainment, and a host of other companies. I knew a lot of people.

Subscribing to the theory that "All it takes is one yes," I sent out a quick email.

?!

Hey, guys . . .

I'm emailing you as friends—I'm thinking about throwing a massive birthday party for myself this summer. I'm turning 30 (ack!!) and was considering doing it in typical "Peter style." That said, if I could get you a proposal as to why this would be a good event for your brand, would you consider donating either product or cash? Let me know . . . of course, you'll be invited. ☺

    Best,

                                   —Peter

?!

Simple, to the point, and quick. Like all of my pitch emails, the key is to get them to read and reply as quickly as possible. The less time that they have to spend thinking about it or "doing something about it," the better your chances for a favorable result. This applies not only to email, but any type of pitch or request. Think about it: what are you more likely to respond to, the email that asks for 20 minutes to discuss the project, or the email that requires a PowerPoint presentation and slide notes to go over the potential feasibility for the next status meeting? Remember Hamburger Man?

Duh.

?!?!?!?!?!?!?!?

> **Rule: Keep it short; keep it simple.**

Not 20 minutes later, the first response:

?!

Hey, Peter—You're so insane! We love it! We love it! How about a bottle of Sebastian conditioner for each attendee? Tell us where to ship.

?!

HAPPY DANCE!

?!?!?!?!?!?!?!?

> **Rule: Learn a happy dance, and when something that warrants it happens, jump out of your chair and happy dance. It's worth it. It kicks up your endorphins and makes you more creative and productive. Think about what Snoopy the dog does—He pats his feet, skips around, and does a happy dance. That's what I'm talking about.**

So we had one on board. This, of course, changed the game entirely.

Now, instead of an email that read, "I'm thinking about doing . . ." the email quickly became:

?!

"Hey, I'm throwing my thirtieth birthday party and I've got a number of sponsors on board—thought you might want to consider joining in. We're going to have a few hundred of the city's top connected people here; it's going to be pretty big. We'll have a logo wall. Media will be there in full force, it's definitely a great way to get your name and image out there. Oh, and I'm not charging for placement! This is a freebie."

?!

Ok. Let's deconstruct the above email.

"I'm throwing this event." People knew it was my birthday party, but hey, anyone can throw a party. This was an "event."

"I've got a number of sponsors on board." Well, one is a number, right? What qualifies as a sponsor? Well, Sebastian was giving me product. That's an "in-kind" sponsor. There are monetary sponsors, too. I didn't have any of those, yet. But they were coming, I hoped.

My logic was simple: if one comes on board, others will follow. And if others didn't follow, then I was fine, too, since Sebastian came on board without any hesitation–they knew they were first, and they took advantage of it anyway.

"We're going to have a few hundred of New York City's top connected people there." This was true. My friends, clients, associates, would all be there. They're more or less quite connected. We tend, as human beings, to associate and hang out with who we know–with those who are similar. It would stand to reason that if I was connected and knew everyone, most of my friends and associates would be to a certain extent, as well.

We'll have a logo wall, translated: "We'll have a place for you to feed your ego, so when you and your bosses walk into the party, you'll see your company's logo in brilliant Technicolor, 15 feet by 15 feet."

"Media will be there in full force." Of course they will. I'm friends with a lot of media. They'd come because I invited them, not because I pitched them. And if one of them finds it interesting and writes something, all the better—but in actuality, it's a party. Come and have fun.

Finally, "Oh, I'm not charging for placement." I'm telling people that normally, they'd have to pay to get their product in front of these types of people—but I'm offering to do it at no charge, as a freebie. That's the call to action they'd otherwise never have.

So what was I really saying? I was letting people know that I was throwing an event. It was going to be big, different, and have the "right" kind of people there. It was going to be an event with caché, with buzz, and a few smart companies were already getting in on the action, realizing that it was a very cheap way to get to their audience.

The target audience was also very important. I don't care what kind of product you're positioning, or where you're based geographically, you need to make sure you're targeting the right audience for your promotion, for your clients, and for your sponsors.

Think about it. I was bringing in the 30-something "cool crowd." Do you think I would have met with much success if I'd pitched Fidelity Retirement Services as a sponsor? Of course not. But what about Yoo-hoo Chocolate Drink? Most definitely. Yoo-hoo was working on promoting their brand to that kind of audience, so it was a perfect fit for them.

?!?!?!?!?!?!?!?

> **Rule: Know your audience, then suggest ideas to the client for ways to improve their basic sponsorship.**

For Yoo-hoo, it was obvious; we would combine their chocolate drink with some form of alcoholic beverage, to make a brand new drink. (For those who are interested: ice, one shot vodka, one shot Kaluha, fill to the top with Yoo-hoo, garnish with a straw–it's called a "HOO-YA!" Quite tasty.)

Yoo-hoo was thrilled, as it let them market to an older crowd, one that might not remember Yoo-hoo from their youth. We got a "signature" drink for the party, and everyone was happy.

We also suggested to Yoo-hoo that they might want to place something into the gift bag that would let people remember them, since drinks are fleeting, at best. They came back beyond our wildest dreams, with full-size Yoo-hoo beach towels. Each person got one, and to this day, people tell me when they use them. ("I was on a cruise, and I brought along my Yoo-hoo beach towel!")

> **Rule:** The goal of an event is not only the press and attention *at* the event, but *after,* as well. Hence the reason the gift-bag business has become a multimillion dollar one. In what kinds of gift bags would your clients or your company fit? Gift bags are an easy win for the client. You should try and include them in a number of different campaigns during various times of the year.

So . . . we're about two months outside the date of my party. Invitation time. Again, rather than the traditional "you are cordially invited to attend" letter, I decided to jazz mine up a bit.

The key to my event was exclusivity–not just anyone could attend this festival. They had to be, for lack of a better word, "cool." Not in the "third grade, you can't sit in the back of the bus because you're not cool" type way, but more along the lines of, as we discussed earlier, "connected." We were looking for people who we knew would actually use their beach towel. We wanted people who would go out the next day and say, "Check this out! I got this at a party I went to last night for my friend's birthday! How cool is this?!"

That's what the majority of my friends are. That's what I was able to play to the media, and more importantly, to my sponsors. I knew that I could get my entire birthday party paid for, and have spectacular gift bags, as long as I could properly convey to those sponsors exactly what my friends were like.

?!?!?!?!?!?!?!?

> **Rule:** Play up what excites you whenever you're trying to pitch something, be it to a client, a reporter, or anyone else. If you believe in it and it excites you, that comes across in how you present! Even the best liar can't present something he doesn't believe in as well as someone who's totally gung-ho over it.

So . . . the invitation. It had to be exclusive. It had to scream "this is my invitation, check it out!" It had to mention the sponsors, show their logos, and be a keepsake.

It had to be something guests would bring with them, then keep with them for the night, then hang up on their desks when they got home.

It had to be . . .

A badge.

Simple, to the point, fun. It would go around your neck, you had to show it to get in. Perfect. People would keep it with them all night, plus, it would lend itself to that "I'm exclusive, I've got a pass!" vibe that the party was starting to take on.

I called a graphic artist I'd used before, and explained what we needed. I explained the exclusivity factor, how it had to look the part, be original, and be something people would want to keep.

?!?!?!?!?!?!?!?

> **Rule:** When you find a vendor you like, whatever he or she does, keep him or her. They're invaluable when you're on a deadline. Pay them on time, respect their work, and you'll have someone to help you for life.

My designer came back with something truly unique, incorporating the sense of urgency and exclusivity I wanted to convey, but also bringing in the fun side, as well. The result, as you see, on the next page.

Front   Back

No way you'd mistake that for a boring or snobbish invitation, huh?

Location: When I started scouting around for different event locations, one that stuck out in my head was brought to my attention by an assistant. The NYC Fire Museum. A four-story building in lower Manhattan, it's one of the hundreds of different museums that no one knows exists in the city.

?!?!?!?!?!?!?!?

> **Rule:** When planning an event, especially if you're no one special and without a million-dollar budget, take an afternoon and go explore. Don't restrict yourselves to the usual places. There are wonders out there, if you're sharp enough to find them.

The space was gorgeous. Not only did my guests have the run of the top floor for the party itself, but they also had the ability to explore the entire museum, seeing fire department memorabilia from years past.

While all of this was going on, boxes were starting to arrive at our office, full of gift-bag product.

> **Rule: Make sure you have room.**

It got to the point where the entire office consisted of desks, boxes, and one walkway connecting the door to the desk. Every other inch of free space was covered in boxes.

Let's take a step back for a second and analyze something.

I'm no one. Ok, I'm not no one, per se, but I'm not Paris Hilton. I'm not Taye Diggs (although with the amount I work out, I should have his abs). Who am I? I'm not famous. I don't star in a reality TV show. I've never released a sex tape (at least, none that I know about).

So what's the deal? Why did over thirty companies trip over themselves to give me product? Why did four companies lay out a bundle of cash to pay for my thirtieth birthday party?

Or, as a reporter for MSNBC so nicely put it, "Peter Shankman, turning 30, the world holds its breath in anticipation. Not."

There was no secret, really. I never claimed to be famous. All I did, quite simply, was craft a good story, a valid story, and position it out to the right people. Using my network of friends and associates, I started the ball rolling, and created a little bit of buzz. From that, I created a little bit more buzz. I then let it carry over on itself. One company asks who else is donating product, I can say a name. They think, "Well, if they're there, we have to be there, too." And then it continues, and continues.

Precis came with six cases of vodka. Why? Because they were just breaking into the American market, and wanted to introduce their vodka to the world.

Good Karmal Chocolates kicked in chocolate for everyone in the gift bags. Why? They were becoming huge on the West Coast, but didn't have a following yet back East.

Sin City Video donated one adult DVD title per gift bag. Over 500 titles in all.

Let's discuss that for a second. Basically, the gift bags had porn in them.

Now is that a huge issue? Well, I suppose it depends on your point of view.

Why did I do it? Well, for starters, one of my largest clients was New Frontier Media, one of the largest distributors of adult pay-per-view on cable. They had donated a lot to the party, both monetarily and in the gift bags. They'd also introduced me to Sin City, who donated the DVDs.

So I did it to recognize them, first of all.

?!?!?!?!?!?!?!?

> **Rule: Recognize the client in public. It makes everyone happy. And it's just good business.**

But I also did it for another reason. Adult entertainment has, over the past ten years, quickly become more mainstream than ever before. Look around! From *Maxim Magazine* to ads in Times Square to *Desperate Housewives* on TV, adult themes and content is everywhere.

It was edgy, it was nontraditional, and it got people talking. Sound like someone you know?

In fact, more people told us after the party that with the possible exception of the Yoo-hoo beach towel, the DVDs were the highlight of the gift bag.

Of course, as soon as we'd confirmed Sin City and the erotic networks as sponsors, we got another call—AstroGlide, the personal body lubricant, was sending 500 bottles. It was getting funnier and funnier by the moment.

Not to be outdone by Sebastian, SAMY Salons sent 500 bottles of Shampoo. All we needed was soap, and people could stay out all night.

A spa in Brooklyn gave 30 percent off coupons.

> **Rule:** Check out smaller places for gift-bag items when you're throwing an event. If you talk to them and explain how it will help them by spreading the word, they're usually the first ones to offer up.

New Frontier Media kicked in gorgeous shot glasses, in addition to a monetary contribution for the event itself.

When all was said and done, the gift bags were worth close to $1,000 a piece. And we had over 400 of them. It was truly, truly insane.

The food, catered by Frambois, an extraordinary caterer out of Staten Island (of all places) was superb, and everyone commented on it.

> **Rule:** Look outside your circle of comfort for vendors. Sometimes, you'll find amazing things where you least expect it. For instance, Staten Island. (See the Resources section for more ideas.)

A week before the party, I drop the *I* bomb. *I*, in this case, stands for Interns.

A word about interns: They are your best friends. They can do more, and are usually *willing* to do more for you than any paid employee almost ever will. Everything to them is grunt work, and they're happy to do it for the experience. Having interns around helps you tremendously.

> **Rule:** Treat the interns right. They're doing most of the really heavy lifting that you don't want to do—make sure they're appreciated. All the interns at
>
> *(continued)*

> my party got to work the party, take home a gift bag, and eat as much as they wanted. They were thrilled.

The interns built the gift bags, helped drag everything over to the space, and in general, did a lot of the final prep busy work that no one ever plans for enough.

> **Rule: Plan for at least half a day extra for busy-work.** This could be anything from making sure there's enough parking to figuring out where to store the beer. But these things will always come up last minute. Make sure you leave enough time to deal with them.

The night before the actual event, try to get some sleep. I know it won't happen, but try anyway. Drink tons of water. While at the party, try to stay away from the alcohol. My employees know they're not allowed to drink until the next day—without fail, the party will be over, everyone will have left, and the second a drop of alcohol touches your lips, the client calls because someone forgot something, or someone's missing something. Just save it, and get drunk the next night.

We'd invited a ton of media, and when they arrived, we got them all settled with what they needed. Being that this was my birthday and I had to do a bit of hosting, I had two employees handling the media at all times, and we were all on radio, so if something happened, I could go right over to them and handle it.

As people started arriving, the flow of the evening took over. We had escorts (former *Penthouse* Pets, actually) escorting bunches of people from the street to the top floor where the party was. They'd walk them in, there was a waiter with Hoo-ya's, complete with Yoo-hoo drink umbrellas—instant branding for Yoo-hoo. They were thrilled, everyone started off with a tasty (and strong!) beverage, a win on all counts. The *Penthouse* Pet would then take about ten people into the elevator, and send them up to the party; they'd get off where they heard the noise. We couldn't have asked for an easier entrance.

We had the Pets in NYC firehouse tank tops, and FDNY shorts. They looked great.

We also invited Rescue 1 to join the party (we'd dropped off invitations earlier in the week). We told them that since they were the firehouse closest to our office, they should stop by. We also told them to bring the truck, if they wanted to.

Sure enough, about halfway through the party, everyone ran to the windows to see the Rescue 1 Fire Truck blaring its lights and siren, as six gorgeous firemen got out, came upstairs, had a drink, shook hands, and posed for photos.

The media loved that, as did all of the female guests.

We overestimated the amount of food we needed, which we always do, deliberately. We'd always rather overestimate than underestimate. One of two things will happen—you'll give it to your employees to take home, or you'll bring it to a mission or homeless shelter and donate it. Either way, it prevents your guests (or worse, your clients) from sitting around going, "Is there really nothing more to eat?"

So let's chat for a second about why. Why this party? Why all the work? Why the insanity of putting it all together?

Well, the classic rules that I live by still apply—I thought it'd be fun.

But of course, there was more. I also thought it might be interesting to see if I could start the ball rolling, and see if it picked up steam. In my case, that ball was corporate sponsorship and product placement.

Could I make enough of a spin out of my birthday (remember, I wasn't famous or anything) to convince over 30 companies to donate product, gifts, and money to make my thirtieth birthday party a success?

"Why did you jump out of that airplane?"

"The door was open."

Why did I throw this party and not have to pay a penny for it? I wanted to see if I could.

> **Rule:** "I wanted to see if I could" is a horrible motto to live by when you're three (I wanted to see if I could shave the cat—never a good one), but it works wonders when you're figuring out new and exciting ways to get publicity.

I wanted to see if it would work. I wanted to see if I could do it. No one else was. No one else, at least, who wasn't famous.

I wanted to see if I could start a trend. I wanted to see if I could convince companies that I was connected enough, that all my friends were connected enough, to drive their products into the right hands.

And it worked.

We were covered by the *New York Times* (full article in the business section), MSNBC, VH-1, and a host of smaller, local media in and around New York. In addition, *Brandweek* picked up on it, as did a bunch of other trade-centric publications.

Of course, this was all eclipsed by seeing close to 450 people in a room, having a good time, enjoying themselves and each other, eating and drinking, and generally having fun, based on nothing more than my suggesting that I wanted to do something fun for my thirtieth birthday.

Oh, that, and trying to explain to my 93-year-old grandmother what AstroGlide was.

WHAT WE LEARNED
FROM THIS CHAPTER

1. "I wanted to see what would happen" is a great, great way to come up with new and exciting ideas.

2. Planning. Who do you know? Who do they know?

3. Who benefits from helping you? What companies benefit from sponsoring your event? Why? That's the pitch you're selling—that they get a lot more out of it than they put in, i.e., a big return on their investment.

4. Don't restrict yourself to the usual places, spaces, or vendors. Explore and leave your comfort zone. See where it takes you and what you get from it.

5. Use one donation as the springboard—allow companies to know who's donating, and see who else comes on board.

6. Be kind to your interns, and they'll work wonders for you.

7. As the days tick off to your event, plan "launch holds" like they do at NASA—specific, planned extra time to take care of problems you don't expect, because they'll always appear.

8. Have fun. It's a party, after all!

?!

CHAPTER 10

What Happens When Your Perfectly Thought-Out Plan Hits a Snag?

I've yet to have a "good" 3 A.M. call. In all my life, I've never had a good phone call that starts at 3 A.M.. They just don't exist.

No one calls you at 3 A.M. to tell you that you're a lottery winner. A supermodel rarely calls at 3 A.M. to profess her love. And I've certainly never gotten the "We want to become your new client" call at 3 in the morning.

The closest thing I've ever gotten to a "good" 3 A.M. call was, "Hello, Mr. Shankman, this is the front desk. Your car is waiting downstairs to take you to the airport. Have a good day."

And even that call pretty much sucked.

So yeah, I think it's safe to say that calls that come in at 3 A.M. are rarely good.

This logic, of course, explains why you never want the phone to ring at 3 A.M. Because when it does, more often than not, it's going to be something like:

Peter, the *LA Times* just came out with their 10-page story on our industry, the one we worked on for three months, and we're not mentioned. At all.

Or:

Peter, the reporter swore to me that we were off the record, and I kind of mentioned our numbers to him, and they're kind of being talked about on CNBC Europe right now.

A personal favorite:

Peter, you're my one phone call from jail. Help.

I've talked with more than one lawyer who prefers me to call them, after the client has called me. Apparently, I have a much more soothing voice than the client who just got hauled into jail on a drunk and disorderly charge.

Let's spend the first half of this chapter talking about what I call "line twists." In skydiving, when you open your parachute, sometimes line twists result. Basically, your parachute is open and flying, but the lines are twisted around. Your job is to analyze the situation, and determine (rather quickly) whether you can kick out of them, or whether you have to cut away and deploy your reserve parachute.

Let's first touch on line twists from which you can kick loose, then we'll follow up with severe line twists, or pure malfunctions, which require you to cut away your main chute and deploy your backup parachute.

Just this morning, I was having breakfast with a client and a reporter. I'd pitched the reporter on my client having a new way to secure *their* client's deposits. The client offers a service in exchange for quite a large sum of money held on deposit, and there were fears within my client's industry that people wouldn't get all of their deposit back.

When I'd called to set up the meeting, the client had given me permission to brief the reporter on this information. The reporter liked the concept, and agreed to the breakfast.

Two days ago, the client called me to let me know that I couldn't talk about the new security feature, as it was being "tweaked." As such, my client couldn't talk about it with the reporter at the breakfast.

Imagine buying a ticket to a Yankees game, and then getting there and being told you weren't allowed to actually watch. Would make it kind of pointless to attend, no?

This situation could have been handled in two different ways:

1. *Not tell the reporter.* Just show up at the breakfast, hope it doesn't come up, smother her with facts and figures and stats and such, and hope that she doesn't have time to ask. If

she does, mumble some excuse about getting her an email soon with details, and aren't these croissants tasty? Or,

2. *Call the reporter up as soon as you find out.* Explain what's going on, that we don't want to give him misinformation, and we certainly wouldn't want him to print inaccurate facts, so let's meet for breakfast anyway since it's near his office and we have the reservation, and we'll give him any information he'd like on anything we can talk about, and as soon as we get the right to speak, he'll be the first one we tell.

Having come this far in the book, you're smart enough to know which option to choose, right?

I opted for the latter choice. The reporter understood, and to his credit, kept the breakfast meeting. He easily could have cancelled it—what does he care? He can always reschedule. But I wanted it to happen; I'd promised the client it would happen.

In the end, the client met with the reporter, told him about upcoming news (not that specific item, but other stuff) traded stories about former jobs and the same people they knew, and the egg-white omelet was quite tasty.

?!?!?!?!?!?!?!?

> **Rule:** Crap happens. Tell the truth, and it lessens the impact. Lying, especially to a reporter, does nothing positive. It will never do anything. It's not helpful. It won't get you any press. And, on the off chance that it does, the slam that will come back to bite you will be so harsh, it will totally and completely annihilate anything good that came out of the lie. It's just not worth it. Be upfront.

> I could never lie. Too many things to remember.
>
> –Anonymous

Here's a great story about why lying is just not worth it: I'm a huge fan of sushi. Always have been. Loved it since I was introduced to it by my first high school crush, Janice, back in 1987.

You've got to have a serious crush on a woman to trust her enough when she says, "Here, try this. It's uncooked octopus."

Anyway, so I'm a fan of sushi. A buddy of mine, starting his own advertising shop, is not.

So, he has a chance to land his first really big client and to seal the deal, he's invited the client and the client's subordinates out for a fancy dinner. Buddy calls me, asks where we should go. I recommend a few different sushi restaurants, thinking "Hey, sushi is cool, it'll work. Get some sake into the client, sign the deal."

My buddy calls me up a few hours later, great, they're on for sushi, and I'm coming. I didn't understand why, until my buddy told me that he'd given the CEO of his potential client all this hype about how great the sushi was here, and how excited he was to take him to "his favorite sushi place," etc., etc., etc.

The CEO bought it, and as luck would have it, is a sushi snob.

My friend was scared out of his mind. He had no idea what to order, how to read the menu, remember–*he'd never had sushi in his life.* As such, I was going as the "Creative Director."

This screamed "Disaster," I told him. Why not just say the sushi place was full, and book an easier restaurant? "No, no. With you there, it'll be fine. Just pick out stuff on the menu for the table, and I'll force myself."

Shrugging, I agreed.

The evening arrives, and we all meet at Tsunami, in Greenwich Village. Great restaurant. I've been many times.

After good conversation (where it really looks like the client wants to sign with my friend), I order. I try to keep it basic, with a few exciting dishes thrown in for good measure. Mostly though, I stick to spicy tuna, toro, California rolls, and the like.

The food arrives. I'd told my buddy that he should just eat exactly what I eat, and he'd be fine. So we start eating off of the giant sushi boats they bring to the table. Spectacular food.

My buddy attempts his first bite . . . gets it down . . . is actually kind of happy with how it tastes! Pretty soon, he's totally fine with it, eating all he can, enjoying it, making great conversation with the client. All is going well.

Until it stops going well. With perhaps three or so pieces of sushi left on the boat, my buddy reaches in for a final piece. "I haven't tried this one yet," he says, to no one in particular.

It was one of those moments where you see what's going on, but your brain can't fully process it right away, and even though neurons and pistons are firing in your head screaming out *DO SOMETHING!* there's nothing you can do. You can just watch in shock, horror, and probably a little bit of amazement . . . as my buddy took the entire ball of wasabi in between his chopsticks, stuck it in his mouth, bit down, and attempted to swallow.

By the time the client and I had realized what was going on (and it couldn't have been more than four seconds, maximum), the color had exploded within his cheeks to a bright reddish/purple. His eyes started to water, and his nose started running.

Of course, my first instinct was to laugh so hard that my head would fall off, but I managed to control myself. I immediately flagged the waiter down, asking for a large bowl of white rice. (With wasabi, water doesn't help. Only rice or something similar, which helps sop up the oil off your tongue, will do the trick.)

My friend was flat out crying now, not intentionally, but the heat of the wasabi was burning his mouth, tongue, esophagus, and probably the interior lining of his throat and stomach.

I really felt for him. I tried to explain to the client that my buddy must have just not been looking, and grabbed the wrong piece off of the plate. Of course, my buddy couldn't do this explaining because, well, at that moment, he couldn't talk.

In about 10 minutes or so, my friend had calmed down enough and eaten enough rice to the point where he could talk again. He profusely apologized for making a scene, blaming it on his hasty eating, and focusing more on the client then on himself. I suggested that it was a case of the shoemaker's kids having no shoes–paying too much attention to the client, never enough to yourself.

The evening ended, and the client (who actually did wind up signing with my buddy, despite his minor malfunction) went one way, and my friend and I went another.

As soon as we were out of earshot, my buddy turned to me: "We should have had Italian, huh?"

I agreed. I said, "You know, you always ask me about karma? You just saw it in action. You lied; you tried to make yourself something you're not. And that's what happened. How's your tongue?"

Postscript: It took my buddy about a week before he could eat anything hotter than "cold." We're still good friends to this day, and I can't see him without saying "WASABI," instead of "What's up?"

Why did he bother, though?

Why do any of us do what Wasabi up there did? Why do we tell the reporter, "I'll get you that info by 5 P.M. today," knowing full well we can't?

I once had a boss who said that too many people over-promise and under-deliver. "The key to being truly successful," he said, "is to do the opposite–under-promise, and over-deliver."

Again, remember Scotty from *Star Trek*. He would always say, "I can fix the ship in three hours," and Captain Kirk would say, "We don't have three hours!" to which Scotty would reply, "I'm doing my best, Captain!"

Of course, Scotty knew it wouldn't take more than five minutes to repair the entire ship. But hey, if you admit to that, then you don't look like a miracle worker!

To truly understand how to get yourself out of line twists, you first need to understand how to avoid almost all of them.

Again, this isn't rocket science. It's basic common sense and logic that for some reason, when we're under pressure, we tend to forget.

Don't make promises you can't keep. "We'll get you the photos by Thursday" should mean, in your mind, "You'll hopefully have them by Wednesday morning, Wednesday evening at the latest."

How many times have we answered a reporter's email with, "Sure, I'll get those facts for you right away." Well, what IS right away? Is it 10 minutes? Tomorrow? Thursday? When's the reporter's deadline?

When was the last time you honestly said, "You know, I don't know. Let me find out for you," as opposed to anything else? As opposed to stretching the truth? As opposed to (horror . . .) making something up?

A mentor once told me that the best answer you can give is, "You know, I don't know the answer to that question, but if you'll let me, I'll make a phone call and find out."

Reporters (any human being, for that matter) will always respect that honesty. It's just life as it happens.

Why make it harder for yourself?

And just so you don't think I'm contradicting something I said a number of chapters ago—there's a big difference between *lying* and *learning*. A client says, "We need to throw a party for 10,000 people. Can you do it?" By answering yes, even if you haven't done it before, you're not lying. If you are sure of your skills, it's not lying. If the client says, "Can you get us onto page 1 of tomorrow's *Wall Street Journal*," and you say, "Yes, most definitely," well, I don't care how good you are. You're lying.

See the difference? It's clear as day. There's no mistaking the two. Embellishing is fine. Flat out making stuff up is not.

A reporter asked me a few weeks ago if I could get him some facts on one of my clients. I asked what he needed, and he said he'd email it over to me that afternoon. I told him that as soon as I got the email, I'd get back to him within 20 minutes with the answers.

His exact response: "Wow, so you're just going to pull those answers out of your ass, huh?"

I was a little surprised—"No," I said. "I'll call the client and get you the numbers you need. Why would I make them up?"

"Because," he said. "Most publicists don't move that fast."

"Oh," I responded. "Well, I was born and raised in New York City. We're a bit faster here."

He laughed, and sure enough, I got him the information in 18 minutes.

It's true, though. Most of us (and yes, even me included sometimes) do the bare minimum. I mean, we live in a country that created the drive-through. I think that gives you some idea.

So the real question becomes, how much more do we have to do to not only prevent problems and line twists, but to become miracle workers?

The answer, surprisingly, is very little. Just be better than the masses, and you'll be remembered. Honestly.

The majority of the time, we expect things to not work in customer service. We expect the dry cleaners to not have our suit ready, and we expect the public laundromat to never fully dry our jeans. We expect that our "Diet Coke with no ice" will usually have ice in it, and we expect that our extra cheese with mushroom pizza will instead have anchovies on it when we get it home and open the box.

Why? Why are we not surprised when something doesn't go right, but pleasantly surprised when it does?

It's how we've been trained. We expect things to not live up to our expectations because they rarely do.

If you exceed those expectations, not only for a client, but for the media, for a specific reporter, or even for the one-time consulting client who you never really liked, you'll be thought of as a hero. But more importantly, you'll avoid line twists to begin with. And that, my friends, is priceless. Looking up at a clean canopy over your head is the greatest feeling in the world. No line twists? Score!

Above and beyond the call of duty. There's a reason they give medals for it.

Now let's talk for a bit about massive line twists, the ones that involve cutting away, or taking other drastic measures to save yourself, your client, and your company.

The majority of issues that produce cutaways in the PR world tend to focus on crisis management, and we've covered that already. So let's focus on the unexpected occurrences that, while not actually crises, can still throw a wrench into things.

Viral: It's not just for penicillin anymore.

Viral marketing is one of the fastest growing segments of marketing today. Don't believe me? Google "Subservient Chicken" and see what I mean. But, with the good can come the bad.

Let's say, for example, that your client's company is named "Acme Auto Parts." Someone buys an oil filter from your client. For whatever reason, it doesn't do the job, and that person's car is trashed.

For $5.00, that guy goes out and buys the domain name "acmeautopartssucks.com" and proceeds to create a 30-second video about why Acme Auto Parts sucks.

What do you do?

Well, before you get all excited and raise your hands to answer, you should know it was kind of a trick question.

If you're smart, you've already registered acmeautopartssucks .com, acmeautopartssux.com, and acmeautopartsblows.com the second you signed the client.

And if you're smart, nothing comes of Mr. Customer having his ride trashed.

Ok, so let's say you're not 100 percent smart, you didn't register the site, and now there's a movie up there.

In the old days, you'd hire a lawyer, sic them on the person, sue for libel, and you're done.

That's because in the old days, things took a lot longer to get out there. In the Internet world, however, they're instantaneous. Don't believe me? Google "Star Wars Kid."

These days what used to be "Release the lawyers!" is now "Come on over for a slice of pizza and a beer, and let's chat."

I know that sounds insane. I know you're thinking, "There's no way I'm going to get the CEO to personally call an irate customer and have a chat with him. That's ridiculous."

Well, let me tell you a quick story.

I'm a very frequent flier, as I've mentioned.

About two years ago, I was finally going to use some miles and head to London for a long weekend with friends. I called up Continental Airlines, and attempted to book the ticket. I figured I'd buy the coach seat, then upgrade using the miles.

Continental hit me with a massive fee to do that.

I was floored. I'm a Platinum traveler! I'm the guy who spends all the money on Continental! I'm not the guy who visits grandma once a year. I was furious.

So I wrote a letter to Continental's CEO, detailing why I was so angry. I explained that I felt like I was being nickel-and-dimed to death, and considering how much I spent with the airline, it didn't really seem right. In fact, it seemed cheap.

Imagine my surprise when two days later, I came back to my office from a meeting and started listening to my voice mails, only to hear this:

"Hi, Mr. Shankman. My name is Larry Kellner, Chairman and Chief Executive of Continental Airlines. I'm in receipt of your letter from a few days ago, and I'd love to talk to you about it. If you have a moment, could you call my direct line?" He then gave me his direct telephone number. Twice.

"Stunned" doesn't even begin to cover it.

I immediately called back, figuring I'd get his assistant—nope. I got HIM. The Chairman and Chief Executive Officer of the sixth largest airline in the world was talking to me on my phone. I was floored.

In the end, he explained the new policy and why it had gone into effect. He waived it for me, apologizing profusely that I didn't get the updated terms and conditions. (I probably did, and more than likely threw them out.)

What does this tell you, not only about the way Continental Airlines does business, but how they handle their PR and crisis management? Guess who's a customer for life, and who continually raves about that experience, even four years later?

That would be me.

The fact is, you still, even in this day and age, catch more flies with honey than with vinegar. Continental realized that I was important to them, and worked to make it right. They did a great job of it, and I still give virtually all of my airline business to them every year.

So back to our auto parts store.

If I owned Acme Auto Parts, and I saw this movie start to gain some traction, I'd have a chat with the customer. I'd call him up, invite him down to the store, and figure out what would make him happy.

I wouldn't have my PR agency email him; I wouldn't have my lawyers send him a letter; I'd do it. Me, personally, the president of Acme Auto Parts. Mr. Acme, himself would make the call.

Why?

Basic. People hate to be wronged, and like to be recognized. People hate knowing that they got screwed over by the Man, but love to know that the man in charge sincerely wants to help them.

Be the man. Work something out. Don't get defensive. Don't get angry. Remember the domain name challenges of a few chapters ago? Everyone who emailed cs@registerfree.com within 24 hours and said they couldn't get online, got a free domain name. Did it cost a few extra dollars? Of course! But did it generate a ton of goodwill, and keep the bad press to a minimum?

You know it did.

In the end, you're looking not only to quell the problem, but find the good solution.

Case in point, a company who didn't find the good solution: Royal Bank of Canada told a long-time customer that because of a new policy, any check drawn on an American bank would have a 25- to 35-day hold on the funds. The man had been banking at Royal Bank of Canada for 13 years. He went to the same branch he'd been going to since he was 9, and the check was from Warner Brothers, not some personal check.

They wouldn't budge, going so far as to tell him that if he wanted better service, he should try another bank.

So he did. But not before going home to his computer. This is where I should mention that he was an animation and Macromedia Flash expert.

Thus, X-Dude versus Royal Bank of Canada, or "The Dough" was born.

View it here: http://www.xdude.com/flashed-mar2001.htm.

It went around the world and back instantly. People came from all over to download it, and Royal Bank of Canada got quite the headache.

Another example? How about "Yours is a very bad hotel."

Tom Farmer and Shane Atchison had confirmed reservations at the DoubleTree Hotel in Houston, Texas. Those reservations weren't honored.

They wrote a PowerPoint presentation, detailing why DoubleTree was such a bad hotel. They sent it on to a few friends. Who sent it on to a few more friends. Who . . . you get the idea. By the time the *USA Today* article on their PowerPoint had come out, hundreds of thousands of people had seen the PowerPoint, DoubleTree had made a charitable donation on their behalf, and their PR people didn't sleep for a month.

According to *USA Today,* they've received several hundred requests from business schools and hospitality companies to use the slide show as an example of "customer service gone horribly wrong."

Perhaps the secret to avoid having a cutaway in the first place is to teach your employees the consequences of their actions. Perhaps that's something we need to focus on as much as crisis management, i.e., being careful enough to avoid most crises before they begin.

In the end, there will be problems, there will be situations that destroy your Friday afternoon or call you back from your vacation. Regardless of how they happened, or what implications they could have, remember the rules.

?!?!?!?!?!?!?!?

> **Rule: Breathe. Stay calm.**

?!?!?!?!?!?!?!?

> **Rule: Breathe: Stay focused.**

?!?!?!?!?!?!?!?

> **Rule: Breathe: Don't waste time blaming. Work the problem, find the solution.**

?!?!?!?!?!?!?!?

> **Rule: Breathe: It's not personal.**

In the end, PR is our chosen profession. And we love it, despite the occasional headaches. Remember: each mistake helps us get better. Each crisis helps us learn how to handle future crises. And remember that the more crises we handle, and the better we get at them, the better we get at anticipating–avoiding–the next crisis before it becomes a crisis.

WHAT WE LEARNED
FROM THIS CHAPTER

1. Problems will pop up, clients will tell you you're allowed to talk about something, then change their minds. Be honest with the reporter, the client, the customer, the stockholders, whomever you're talking to. It'll save you a world of trouble in the future, and in the end, it'll help you. Promise.

2. Boasting to try to improve yourself will never work. Boasting about what you're good at isn't lying, it's telling the truth. Boasting about something you're totally and completely unfamiliar with (like sushi) will only come back to bite you.

3. If you make a promise, keep it. "We'll get you an interview with the client by Thursday" means Wednesday at the latest.

4. Under-promise and over-deliver.

5. How are you preventing the problems from happening in the first place? Are you talking to the right people, reserving the right domain names, making sure clients are happy on a random basis?

6. If you think no one will pick up on the dissatisfied customer's rant, think again. Make him happy before he has a chance to spread the rant.

7. If you can't or didn't make the customer incredibly happy at first, make sure the world knows that you've since made him ecstatic.

8. Breathe. It's not personal.

?!

CHAPTER 11

Putting It All Together

So you're on the last chapter! Congratulations! How does it feel? Know a lot more now than you did? Enthralled? Still awake?

So what did you learn? Hopefully, I've given you a few insights on PR, stunts, and how to relate to the media. But more importantly, I hope I've given you a little insight into how to think differently.

See, if you take anything at all away from this book, let it be that the key to success in PR, in marketing, heck, in virtually anything, is allowing yourself the option of thinking differently. There are sheep and then there are leaders. The sheep tend to think along the same lines as everyone else. The leaders make the lines in the first place, and while the sheep are following them, the leaders go and change the lines.

Here's a test for you. When was the last time you took a different route to work for no other reason than you felt like it? Not, "I-278 is jammed, I'll take the local streets," but "You know, I think I'll take the road down by the river today. I know it leads somewhere close to my office; I'll figure it out. It'll be a nice change of pace."

A nice change of pace. Isn't that what we're all looking for? Isn't that what reporters are looking for, too?

Instead of sending out a release that talks about how the new office is finished and you've got 20 employees and you're very excited about your growth, wouldn't it be a nice change of pace to have a moving party and invite all the local townspeople to help you, and then have a huge fried chicken dinner? How about it?

And wouldn't it also be a nice change of pace if that wound up being the lead in the business section of your local paper? All because you tried something different? You weren't a baboon, a sheep.

It's funny. Back in school, when we were all kids, we were taught that there's work time and there's play time. Remember? You'd do your math problems so you could get to what? Recess, of course. You'd work all morning, just knowing that recess was right around the corner, and recess, well, hey, recess was FUN! Recess was letting off steam, enjoying yourself, laughing, smiling, and all the other things you weren't really "allowed" to do during the rest of the day, while you were (shhhh!) "working."

Now forgive me. I'm a relatively smart person. (I have to be! I'm writing a book!) But I simply don't get it.

WHY IS WORK NOT ALLOWED TO BE FUN?

What idiot came up with this rule? Who in their right mind would come up with a rule that basically says, "Ok, you're going to be spending, at minimum, 45 hours a week doing something, but you're not allowed to love it!"

WHY IS THAT?

And we bought it! We've bought into this like it's some natural thing! What were we thinking?

How many times have you heard your friends say (or you've even said yourself), "Oh, I work so I can get a paycheck so I can enjoy myself when I'm not working."

Forgive me, but I'm here to say that the previous sentence is probably one of the stupidest I've EVER heard, except perhaps for the publicist who tried to promote a brand of soup after the tragedy of 9/11 by saying, "What the world needs now is the comfort food that is soup."

Come on, people. How can we possibly expect to do any quality work, come up with any stellar ideas, pitch any original stories, or do anything else of any value in our professional lives, if we can't even get passionate about what we do for a living?

Basically, it comes down to a quote I heard a few years ago. This struck me, and I offer it to you:

> If you can't change the people around you, change the people around you!

Translated: If you're in a rut, and can't get out of it, and aren't producing the quality you know you can, and can't figure out how to change it, maybe it's time to look for different scenery.

How many times (and I'm guilty of this too) do we say, "Oh, I'm just in a rut," or "I'm just spinning my wheels."

Why do we allow that to keep happening to ourselves? Why don't we realize that there are ways to get out of those ruts, ways to regain traction and get back on the road?

And to venture off for a second, because I'm sure some of you are asking, "What does this have to do with PR?" the answer is "Everything."

What's your day like? You get into the office, sit down, get some coffee, check email, work, write a pitch or two, get some lunch, pitch some more, get a snack, eat jelly beans, answer more email, blah, blah, blah.

Why? And don't you DARE say, "Because that's the way we've always done it." I'll reach right through this book and smack you.

The fact of the matter is, we put ourselves into ruts. We do! We settle into routine because it's comfortable. We take the expressway the same way to work each day because it's easy. We go to the burger place on the corner instead of the health food store because it's a block closer. We are trained to take the easy way out. And that's fine for some things.

If I have two dry cleaners in my neighborhood, and both are the same price and do the same job, but one is a block from my apartment and one is six blocks across town, of course I'm going to use the one next to my apartment. And that's fine! That's perfectly understandable!

The problem, however, is when we do the same thing in all facets of our lives. Because we then become complacent. Complacency, as I've said many, many times, can lead to failure.

?!?!?!?!?!?!?!?

> **Rule: If you become complacent, you tend to do things the easiest possible way. This is not always the right way.**

Why did you send out that normal, boring pitch that no one is going to answer? "Oh, I couldn't think of anything different to pitch them on."

Good thing you're not a doctor! "Oh, I couldn't get motivated enough to do a triple bypass, so I just did a double. It *should* work."

?!?!?!?!?!?!?!?

> **Rule: Complacency and ruts are similar to thirst. By the time your brain tells you, "Hey, you're thirsty—go get a drink of water," you're already partially dehydrated. By the time you stop and think, "Hey, I could be slowing down—maybe I'm in a rut and need a change," you're already there.**

I'm going to present 5 + 1; that is, five rules plus one more rule to stir up some creativity:

?!?!?!?!?!?!?!?

> **Rule 5: Read differently: For an entire day, read someone else's blog subscriptions, someone else's magazines, someone else's books. Find out what they're reading. Understand why they're reading it. Learn something new. Come away with a different take on something, even if it's just a fact about the latest celebrity you didn't know before. Then go back and figure out how to incorporate that into your next pitch.**

Rule 4: Sweat differently: Work out already? Good. Switch up your routine. Instead of going to the gym, doing a few lame trunk twists then getting on the elliptical machine for 30 minutes while watching a rerun, take a class. Or go for a run in the park, or even take a class or program outside your comfort level, taught by someone new. (See the Resources pages for more ideas.) The key is to come up with different ideas while doing new things. Plus, you'll get in better shape. How is that a bad thing?

Rule 3: Travel differently: Look for new ways to go to work. Subscribe to an airline's "last minute" fares email, and go to a beach for the weekend. Bring a notebook; write down whatever comes to you.

Rule 2: Eat differently: They say that a new diet can change your entire outlook. Meat eater? Give it up for a week—eat only vegetables and tofu for protein. Love pizza? Dump it in favor of health food. Coffee junkie? Switch to decaf for a week. See what happens.

Rule 1: Finally, associate differently: Join a club, meet some new people— not work related. Explore a hobby. I joined a kickball league last summer. I made some new friends, had fun, learned that I truly suck at kickball, but got some fun times out of it, and a few new stories.

Rule +1: Try everything at least once.

Ok. What does any of this have to do with stunt-driven PR?

Well, in a nutshell—you ain't gonna come up with those ideas sitting behind your desk all day!

My dad took me fishing once. I was, I think, ten years old or so. I hated it. Couldn't sit still in the boat, got way too bored, way too fast. I kept reeling in and recasting, reeling in and recasting, with no success.

Finally, I shouted out, "I hate this. I can't catch any fish." The friend of my dad's who was on the boat with us turned to me and said, "Son, if you want to catch fish, your hook needs to be in the water."

In other words, if you want to be creative, you have to do things that inspire creativity!

Did you know there are over 1,000 blogs that came up in a search on "Knitting?" And there are over 10,000 that came up via a search on "Celebrity."

What don't you know? Go search it out and read about it for an hour.

Read biographies! Check out famous people who you admire. Learn about them. More importantly, learn why you admire them! Then adopt what they do! One famous person said he "always takes the first meeting." So I do, too.

Let's talk for a second about mentors. First off, I believe that everyone should have one. I've been incredibly fortunate to have two since I started my first agency, and they've both been invaluable to me.

Find someone you respect, someone you trust, and someone who won't worry that you're trying to steal their job, and work with them. Invite them to lunch. Pick their brain. Ask questions. Read up on them. Figure out what they're doing that other people think is weird. Find out why they're doing it, and try it yourself.

There's a line from the movie *Point Break* that says: "It's not tragic to die doing something you love."

I'll recreate that line, a little bit less cheesy, though:

It's not tragic to flame out on an idea you thought was brilliant.

Or, I'll let someone who is quoted a lot say it best:

A great deal of talent is lost to the world for want of a little courage. Every day sends to their graves obscure men whose timidity prevented them from making a first effort.

–Sydney Smith, famous English writer and clergyman

Take the chance. The worst that can happen is that you fail. And failure is what lends experience to your next success.

Here's a great skydiving quote passed down from the older "Sky Gods" to the new kids just aching to get up in the air:

> Good judgment comes from experience. Experience comes from watching other people implement bad judgment.

Don't be the other person, but on the same note, don't be afraid to fail, as long as you promise yourself that you'll learn from the failure. Failure is actually a great thing. It allows us to learn, if we let it. If we let failure teach us, we can be incredibly smart. Find that middle ground between comfortable experience and taking the risk.

How many times do you email a reporter after he or she has turned you down on a pitch and ask why? Try it! Just a quick email—I send them out all the time:

?!

Dear Reporter . . . (yes, I use the person's name):

I noticed you wrote a story on <insert client's industry here>. I'd sent you an email about a month or so ago with my client's information, yet we weren't included in the story.

I'm not asking for anything, I'm just trying to learn a bit—was there a specific reason we weren't included? If it was simply space, that's totally understandable, and hopefully we'll make it next time. But if it was something else, I'd love to know. It would help me out in the future, and with any luck, even make the pitches I send to you easier and more tailored to what you're looking for.

Feel free to send me as much or as little as you'd like—every little bit helps. I thank you so much for taking the time.

All the best,

Peter Shankman

?!

I get a ton of responses from emails like that one. Sometimes, the reporters just didn't even get to my original email, they were so swamped. Other times, they just forgot to mention us, and still other times, they didn't understand why we were important. Those are the responses that matter—the ones that help us change our pitch and our ideas of how we pitch. Those are the responses that help us do our jobs better.

?!?!?!?!?!?!?!?!

> **Rule: Ask questions. No one ever died asking a question. In my company, I'll never yell at you for asking a question as many times as you need to. If you don't ask the question and then you screw something up, though, you're buying lunch for the entire office. For a week.**

Why wouldn't you ask questions? Questions are the easiest "free pass" in the world. So many people do so many things wrong because they simply don't ask questions. Sometimes it simply amazes me.

Questions also show that it's not just all about you. When you ask someone a question (I mean a real question, not "So . . . how about those Yankees?"), you're expressing interest in their life. You want to know what's going on in their world. You're asking to be let in, and asking to be trusted. This is a bond that few publicists and media people take the time to really work on creating anymore, and it's kind of sad. In this world of email, IM, and immediacy, it has sort of fallen by the wayside.

Something to think about the next time you're talking to a reporter, or an editor. Remember that these people have lives outside of work, and that asking about them is not only a nice thing to do, but might lead to a new friend, activity partner, or more. You never know, unless you try.

Ever wonder why some publicists tend to get better responses from their reporters more often than you do? I look at it as sort of a relationship. And like any relationship, it can't always be about you. Quite frankly, it needs to be less about you by a wide margin, and so much more about the reporter, or the editor, or the publisher, or the producer.

Think about it this way. There are two guys who primarily deliver take-out to the office. One is a really nice guy, brought his family over several years ago, supports them while going to school, does the delivery thing during the day, is a waiter at night. I've seen photos of his kids; he tells me when the restaurant is getting in new foods, etc.

The other delivery guy is a very nice guy, always delivers my food hot.

Which one do you think I'm going to write an INS recommendation letter for?

In the end, we work in an industry that lives or dies on relationships. And those relationships make or break every stunt you pull, every request for coverage you want, and every inch of column space you crave. It's really that simple.

Now let's talk a little bit about luck.

Thomas Jefferson once said, "I'm a great believer in luck, and I find the harder I work, the more I have of it."

I'm inclined to believe him. Fortune favors the bold. Take those chances, and you'll find that luck tends to be on your side. Of course, it also helps to be intelligent and to make wise choices. But I've found that at least in my career, if I thought all my good fortune was because I was good, and none of it was because of luck, I'd be kidding myself.

Think about it the next time you're doing a stunt. If it's an outdoor stunt, the easiest way to think about it is the weather:

If you're lucky, you'll get a gorgeous day for your event.

If you're lucky AND good, you've reserved a back up spot in case it pours.

If you're lucky, it's a slow news day.

If you're lucky AND good, you've figured out three or four different back-stories for follow-up in case something major breaks.

If you're lucky, the celebrity you hired has gotten into a huge catfight the day before, and now she's major news.

If you're lucky AND good, you've secured media coverage beforehand so regardless of what she's up to, you're Ok.

See the goal here? Let's put it another way: You start off with an empty bag of experience and a full bag of luck. Your job is to fill the bag of experience before emptying the bag of luck.

How? Well, I find that you can continually create luck by relying on the experiences you've had. Once you master that, you'll never really empty the whole bag of luck.

For instance, if you find that you're a really good "stunter" (i.e., you can come up with the best ideas in the world), but you're not necessarily the best person to implement them (i.e., you're not truly a "details" person), then maybe teaming up with someone who is a detail person might be the best course of action for you.

If you can go in and wow the client every single time with your brilliant ideas, and then know that you've got someone (or a team of someones) you can rely on to help turn those brilliant ideas into reality, then you've taken your own experience (your ability) and added in your own luck (your knowledge that you need someone to help you out).

Your goal should always be (among the many others you're tasked with on a daily basis) to figure out how to make your own luck–the wisest man is the one who realizes that he can't do it entirely on his own.

Example of me not knowing this:

I was planning a trade show media tour for a client. I'd never been to this particular city before, so I went onto a mapping program online and figured out that a certain hotel was less than a quarter-mile from the convention center. Perfect, I thought. If I book a suite here, we can get all the reporters to come over to the suite, either before or after the show, or even during the middle of the day, have a drink, relax, and we'll get all the interviews done that way.

So I did it. I booked a huge suite, catered it, the whole nine yards.

Upon getting to the convention center, I dropped my bag at our booth, and decided to walk the route myself, right to our hotel suite.

It was, in fact, a quarter-mile from the convention center. Unfortunately, to get through that quarter-mile, you had to negotiate a six-lane highway. The one road that led directly to the hotel? You guessed it—no pedestrians allowed.

Six of the nine reporters cancelled their meetings with me, rather than deal with the hassle of a 30-minute cab line.

Did I ever book another suite without talking to at least seven people who lived in the city, worked at the convention center, or somehow knew the city back and forth? Not a chance.

I learned my lesson. I took out a few ounces of luck, and replaced them with a lot of experience.

It's how we grow.

A lot of times, I stop and ask myself, "Why are these companies paying me? Why are they trusting me to get them press, make a name for them, get them differentiated from their competitors? Why me, as opposed to someone else?"

Perhaps I try harder? Perhaps I'm wackier? Maybe I have better ideas? Maybe they can't afford a giant agency. I don't know. What I do know, though, is that a client brings me on board to do a job, and that job involves me being creative, and reaching into my brain and pulling out my experience—all that I've gained; from other clients, from mentors, from reading newspapers, from watching TV, from running, from walking down the stairs, from petting my cat, from skydiving—from anything and everything I've done in my life.

The human brain is an amazing organ, and it can do so much more if we let it. Your job (among others, again) is to LET IT!

You must live in the present, launch yourself on every wave, find your eternity in each moment.

–Henry David Thoreau

Henry had it right there. Everything you do, from reading this book to where you ate dinner tonight has implications on how you work, how you become creative, how you do things differently than the masses. Our brains are like giant digital video recorders. They record everything they see. The filing system though, could probably use a little work. So try to remember everything. Try to focus on what you did today; then tomorrow, do it just a little bit differently.

Try to cross-reference. It goes something like this:

"We need a crazy idea for a client in 20 minutes!" Ok. Let's see. Well, the client makes running sneakers. Ok. Sneakers run on pavement, on concrete, in the woods, in the jungle . . . hmmm. . . . Ok, sneakers run on the concrete jungle. Ok, well, a concrete jungle is any major city. Ok, how do we use that? Well, what if we took over a city block somewhere and turned it into a giant climbing jungle? Or a jungle gym! Remember jungle gyms? Yes! Let's release the kid in all of us. Maybe that's the tagline! "Release the kid in you." Running, playing . . . let's make it a giant jungle gym and bring back recess.

RECESS! Let's bring back recess! Let's make a RECESS during lunch! We'll get all these worker-bees to come downstairs out of their offices, give them sneakers, and let them play tag! YES! GROWN-UP TAG!! THAT'S IT! Using our sneakers! This is awesome! The corporate world's first ever game of tag! Welcome to Creative Brainstorming 101.

Never lose your creativity. Never attempt to squash it. Invite other people to take part in it, as well!

We invite reporters over all the time to hang out, eat pizza, and brainstorm with us. We ask them what they want in a PR person, what they want in a story. We listen . . . we talk . . . it works.

Never squash creativity. It's bad PR karma.

More than anything, I've tried to explain here that PR, events, stunts, and yes, even creativity, must be fostered in an environment of happiness, positive energy, and excitement.

If you're not in an environment like that, then you have to ask yourself if you're in the right environment at all. That, more than anything else, is the key first step. Are you in an environment that encourages creative thinking, allows you to "do things differently," and actually encourages you to take chances? If not, ask yourself if it's time to be someplace else.

Time for another story.

I once had a professor in college who taught a really tough photography class. Nothing I ever did in that class ever came close to being right. He'd tell us to "go be creative," and we'd go out and shoot our hearts out, only to develop and print the film and find that it wasn't very creative at all—in fact, it was downright mundane.

One day, on a Saturday morning, I found myself in the enviable position of not having any work due. This was a rarity for me, as I'm a brilliant procrastinator. But I had nothing to do! No assignments due, nothing on the agenda for the entire weekend.

So for kicks, I grabbed my camera, and went for a walk.

I walked around for hours, just taking random photos of random things. . . . I wasn't really looking for any specific shots; I wasn't trying to capture that awesome moment. I was just shooting for pleasure.

I got home, put the camera down, and enjoyed the rest of my weekend. The following week, I went into the darkroom and developed my photos.

You can see where this is going, I'm sure. I found some truly spectacular pictures on that roll! Things I never thought of taking on my own, things I never assumed could come out of my brain, were showing up on my negatives.

I was thrilled! But for the life of me, I couldn't figure out why. Why now? I was almost angry! Why now, after I've been busting my butt for months in this professor's class, does all my work suddenly take on this flair that I never knew existed within me?

I was really, really frustrated, and even more so the next week, when I shot another assignment for class and it came out, yet again, quite mediocre.

I was talking to my mom about it a few days later. She started laughing when I mentioned how angry I was getting.

"Why are you laughing? It's not funny," I shouted.

"Actually, it is, Peter. What you're saying to me is that you're a good photographer, you just don't seem to be a good photographer under the current conditions."

Good old Mom. Always right when I need her to be.

And she was right. It wasn't that I was terrible, it's that under those conditions, I wasn't doing my best work.

Well, once I realized that, I was able to separate the two, and of course, take some amazing photos. At least, I thought they were amazing.

So what are my final rules?

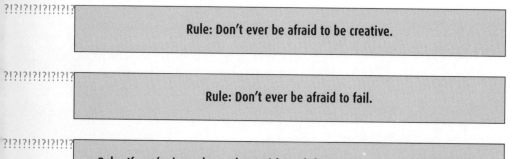

?!?!?!?!?!?!?!?

Rule: Don't ever be afraid to be creative.

?!?!?!?!?!?!?!?

Rule: Don't ever be afraid to fail.

?!?!?!?!?!?!?!?

Rule: If you're in a place where either of the two previous rules can't happen, ask yourself if you're really meant to be there.

So perhaps that's the answer—look into yourself. When you get frustrated, or feel like there just aren't any fresh ideas out there, perhaps the key is a little bit of change. And it doesn't always have to be drastic. I'm not saying you should tell the boss to "take this job and shove it" every time you have a momentary lapse of creativity.

But, if you've read this book the whole way through, maybe you'll try a few of the ideas I've suggested. Maybe you'll go for a run, or try something that scares you, or give up pasta for a week. Maybe you'll take a trip, or buy a new suit . . . or do something different. Something that excites you. Something that creates a new neural pathway in your brain, through which new ideas and new creativity can flow.

While it truly is one of the best feelings in the world to conceive of the idea, implement it, and laugh like a giddy child when it works beyond your wildest dreams, remember that those successes are just steps on a much longer road. And on the same note, when an idea blows up into a massively brilliant failure, and you learn from that failure, that too, is just another step on the road.

Everything we do—every flash of brilliance we have, every "crazy idea" we conceive, and every "nah, that'll never work" thought that we're able to beat down is yet another step on our creative journey. And those steps are what make the whole thing so much fun.

Perhaps the real treasure isn't waiting for us at the end of the road, but rather, is comprised of the experiences we have as we travel the road itself.

Happy, creative, exciting, and wonderful travels.

?!

CHAPTER 12

The Resources Section!

Now honestly . . . what good would any book on doing outrageous PR be, if there wasn't a resources section to get you started!

The following links are places online I go to get creative, get help, get a nice "kick-in-the-butt," etc. They come in handy when I'm stuck, or when I just need a mental distraction to hurdle a roadblock.

I've broken them down into sections, including "helpful," "fun," "noncomputer," and others. Happy exploring!

GOOGLE

Everyone knows Google, but did you know what *else* Google can do?

- http://www.google.com (Basic Google Site)–Best tip I can give you is the + and – signs. Say, for instance, I want to do a search on a reporter named Tom Hanks. That would be really annoying, huh? Imagine the results you'd have to wade through. But, if you type in "Tom Hanks – movie – movie star – Hollywood" then you can considerably narrow down your results. In other words, you're telling Google to search "Tom Hanks," but to disregard all matches if they have movie, movie star, or Hollywood anywhere in them. This comes in really handy. If Tom Hanks the reporter only covers rocketry, you can pretty much bet that "movie star" won't be in his story.

- http://toolbar.google.com—This is a little toolbar that sits atop your browser. It lets you search right from the browser, no matter what website you're on. Good when you're reading something and want more info on it ASAP.
- http://news.google.com—Awesome. Enter a reporter's name, see what he or she has written about in the past. Also, put quotes around the reporter's name ("Martha Irvine") and it will only find that phrase (as opposed to: "In Irvine, California, today, Martha bought a latte.")
- http://trends.google.com—This is a fun one. This lets you see how a term ("stock market," for instance) holds up against the news on it—spiking in demand and ebbing when it's not that important. Gives you an idea of what stories are important when, so you can tailor your pitching time-wise, accordingly. Try it!
- http://www.google.com/alerts?hl=en (Google News Alerts)— This should be used by EVERYONE reading this book. It's easy, and it's free. Simply enter a search term ("Peter Shankman" for instance) and Google emails you immediately whenever that term hits the news, or a new space on the Web. Awesome for finding stories that just came out on your client that you can then email directly to the client, and look brilliant.

BLOGGITY, BLOG BLOG

Ok, blogs. We've got to talk about them at some point.

Here's my list. Take it with a grain of salt. Remember, for every opinion out there, there are a few hundred bloggers who think their opinion is better. And if you still disagree with them all, start your own!

For creating your own blogs, I'm a fan of Typepad. That's what I use—www.typepad.com—it costs a few bucks, but it's worth it.

Blogger (www.blogger.com) is free, and almost as good. Good place to start if you don't want to spend the money.

In terms of how I read my blogs, try BlogLines (www.bloglines .com), a free service that keeps all your blogs in one place, and also lets you download a little file that sits in your Windows taskbar and updates you when any of the things on your list get updated. Great for distraction. I recommend shutting it off most of the time, though, lest you wind up getting zero work done.

I'll start with my top-five most recommended in PR, then expand from there. These aren't in any particular order, other than how I have them listed in my Bloglines search, so no inferring, please.

5. Steve Rubel runs MicroPersuasion (www.micropersuasion .com)–it's a good overall read about the world of PR and how it intersects the tech world of the Web. Worth tracking.

4. Phil Gomes is a savvy, very "in the moment" publicist. He's extremely tech savvy, usually has the latest on products, and knows from what he speaks. Find him at www.philgomes .com/blog.

3. Colin McKay writes CanuckFlack (http://www.canuckflack .com)–a worthy daily check-out. Also Internet/PR based, but has a really good smattering of all facets of PR. Plus, Colin has a quirky sense of humor. Recommended.

2. Constantin Basturea produces PR meets the WWW (http://blog.basturea.com)–and has some really interesting PR commentary. It's nice to expand outside your typical "three-foot-circle," as I call it. Constantin also organizes the PR Blog list–the sort of "master list" of all PR Bloggers.–http://www.bloglines.com/public/prblogs.

1. Finally, Tom Murphy hosts "PR Opinions" at http://www .natterjackpr.com–Good read, plus a good list of sites that have quality reading as well.

   Oh yeah, plus one–mine–

+1. www.prdifferently.com–A twist on PR, I try and keep it interesting, funny, and 98 percent on topic. Most of the time, I get there.

As I mentioned, if you use Bloglines, you can set up your blogs in specific categories. Here's how mine look:

The folders each contain various blogs, and when I open each one, I get to view all my blogs, both read and unread. Whenever I click onto one of them, I can see what I've read, what I haven't yet read, and how many unread items there are in each blog. It's really helpful, but like I said, if you have a lot of blogs, you're going to want to shut off the notifier, or you'll never get any work done.

**Some definite Bloglines requirements
for anybody in PR:**

News

www.fastcompany.com

www.salon.com

www.news.com

http://business2.blogs.com/business2blog

www.slate.com

www.boingboing.net

Gossip

www.perezhilton.com

www.asocialiteslife.com

www.idontlikeyouinthatway.com

www.dlisted.com

I call the following "Mandatory Blogs," because we should all check them once a day, mostly because they tend to get big scoops which, if you work in media, government, or entertainment, are important, and even if you don't might spur your brain into a new way of thinking.

www.wonkette.com (Washington, DC, gossip)

www.drudgereport.com (A lot of people think he's an idiot, but he occasionally nails a breaking news or exclusive item that no one else gets until later. Worth a once-a-day check-in.)

www.defamer.com (Hollywood gossip)

www.gawker.com (New York and media gossip)

www.lifehacker.com (Tools to make you more productive. Very helpful.)

http://www.quotationspage.com/qotd.html (Quotes of the day)

http://www.snopes.com–You know those "Forward this email to 1,000 people and you'll get a million dollars" emails you get? These guys tell which ones are real and which are fake. GREAT website. Shuts your annoying friends up really fast.

WHAT DOES THAT MEAN?

General

Wikipedia (http://www.wikipedia.org) is a wonderful user-generated encyclopedia, covering everything that anyone deems important. Over 1,500,000 articles, it's totally free to search, and you can even add your own. This is helpful if your clients start getting lots of media attention, and you want to move it up to the next level. It's peer-rated, so if you're full of it, you'll be called on it.

PR-Specific

I fell in love with the Young PR Pros list about five years ago. As one of the co-owners, I still say it's one of the best PR resources out there. Join it at (www.youngprpros.com). It's an email community of some of the brightest young minds in the PR world. If that doesn't suit your fancy, go to groups.yahoo.com and type in "Public Relations." You'll get enough to keep you busy for ages.

How many times are you trying to book a celebrity, and have no idea where to go to find out how to contact them? Who Represents? is a great service, despite a poorly thought-out URL– www.whorepresents.com–and no, it doesn't mean WHORE PRESENTS.

While it costs a lot, Media Map Online (www.mediamap .com online) has listings of every single journalist in the world, and contact info for them. It's one of those sites you just know you need, despite how damn expensive they are. However, here's a tip: find nine friends, and Media Map will let you go in on a co-op, allowing you to all have your own logins to the service, but split the cost ten ways. So a year of service comes out to under $1k a piece. Score!

Ever wonder how so many idiots seem to get into the paper quoted as experts on an almost daily basis? Usually they use a service called Profnet. It's a journalist lead program, where about seven or eight times a day, you'll get an email with requests from lots of different reporters from news organizations all over the globe, ranging from the typical (I need a source who can tell me what they think is going to happen in the latest Microsoft trial) to the obscure (I need someone who is familiar with which part of the Bolivian army ant is edible, and which is poisonous) to the truly odd (Have you ever been dumped by a guy so to get back at him, started dating his father? I'm a reporter for a woman's magazine looking to do a piece on this.)

It's a worthy investment, if you're a solo practitioner; it's also rather cheap (www.profnet.com).

VMS: If you think you're going to be on TV, or you know you're going to be on TV, don't blow it after you're on TV by sending out crappy video to your client. VMS captures and sends you the actual clip, and will put cool little titles in it for you. It's worth it. I use them (http://www.vidmon.com).

TV Eyes: If you're as ADHD as I am, check out TV Eyes. They use computers and voice analysis to monitor, real time, what is said on various newscasts. Very cool, if not slightly terrifying (www.tveyes.com).

I WANT TO TALK TO YOU NOW!

There are about 45,000,000 instant messaging programs out there, and they pretty much all do the same thing. Problem is, if you're on Yahoo! Instant Messenger, and I'm on AOL Instant Messenger, we're not communicating. Fortunately, that's solvable.

If you've any desire to get in touch with me via any of the services, feel free, I'm:

AIM: Pshankman
Yahoo: geekfactory
MSN:IM: peter@shankman.com
ICQ: 4512996
Gmail/GoogleTalk: Geekfactory
Skype: GeekFactory

Trillian takes all the various platforms (AOL, Yahoo!, MSN, ICQ, IRC, Jabber, and GoogleTalk) and puts them all on one platform. Lifesaving (www.trillian.cc). Regular is free, $30 or so to upgrade. Upgrade, it's worth it. Also does seamless video and audio chat.

Skype lets me talk to people when I'm overseas (or anywhere, really, but I mostly use it overseas) on VOIP (Voice over IP)—in other words, I dial a regular phone number and talk into my computer. It's pennies per call. A heck of a lot cheaper than international cell phone rates—(www.skype.com). A lot of other companies (Google, Yahoo!, etc.) are doing this now, so look around.

WHAT TO READ

I read three PR pubs, primarily, and only one is paper (*PRWeek*):

Holmes Report
O'Dwyer's PR Daily
PRWeek

That will pretty much give you everything you need from the PR world.

WHAT TO READ OUTSIDE OF PR

This pretty much comes down to personal preference but I find, more than anything, the following publications tend to pop up in PR people's mailboxes more often than not:

Time

Newsweek

Entertainment Weekly

People

Us

Vanity Fair

Details

GQ

Vogue

Cosmopolitan

Radar

BusinessWeek

U.S. News and World Report

The *New York Times*

The *Wall Street Journal*

The *Washington Post*

The *Los Angeles Times*

Fortune

The *New Yorker*

New York

OK! and *Hello!* (Both from London, bigger newsstands carry them)

The *Chicago Tribune*

There are tons and tons of others, but those are a few of the majors. Like I said, mostly it will come down to who you're working for, where you live, and what you're pitching.

To quote Homer Simpson, "Why do they put all this crap in my newspaper? World. Arts. Religion. Ah, here we go . . . [pulls out section entitled 'Kickin' Back–50 Ways to Waste Your Weekend']."

It really comes down to preference.

FINALLY, GET ME OUT OF THIS OFFICE!!

You need a break, right? You need to stop looking at client work and take a few minutes of personal time. Even if you can't leave the office, the following should help:

www.skydivingmovies.com   Go log in and download a few clips of people jumping out of (or off of) high things. This will raise your adrenalin without you having to actually do anything.

www.popcap.com   Tons of games to get you hyped up. I'm partial to bookworm, myself.

www.uspa.org   Go find a drop zone and jump out of a plane! It will change your life. If you can handle that, coming up with new ideas for clients should be a breeze.

www.runtheplanet.com   Go for a run. It will up your endorphins, teach you to think better, problem solve better, and all-around do things in a more outside-y way. Run the Planet helps you find running buddies, anywhere in the world.

http://www.gorillamask.net   Fun timewaster of different movies, videos, updated hourly.

www.cuteoverload.com   This will suck all your time, and you'll go "awww" way too much. It's exactly what it sounds like. Pictures of puppies, kittens, babies, etc. I can go for about three minutes before I need something manly again.

www.airtroductons.com   The next time you're flying, jump on here to find a seatmate. Who knows? Could open up a whole new world for you!

Finally, did I miss anything? Let me know. Email me and I'll be happy to reply! Find me at The Geek Factory (peter@geekfactory.com).

INDEX

?!